A 'D IVING
COMPL N ABOUT

CW01630622

# BE YOUR OWN DOCTOR WITH

# MAGNET THERAPY

*by*

Dr. Dhiren Gala
B.Sc., D.H.M.S., D.O., D.Ac.,
C.G.O., C.C.H., A.R.S.H.
Recipient of a gold medal for extraordinary work in the field of Alternative Therapeutics

*With*

Dr. D. R. Gala
N.D., D.N.O., D.C.O.

Dr. Sanjay Gala
M.B. (BOM.), M.S. (ENT)

Price : Rs. 25.00

NAVNEET

**NAVNEET PUBLICATIONS (INDIA) LIMITED**

| **Navneet House** | **Navneet Bhavan** |
| --- | --- |
| Gurukul Road, Memnagar, Ahmadabad – 380 052. | Bhavanishankar Road, Dadar, Mumbai – 400 028. |
| Phone : 745 10 00/743 63 00 | Phone : 430 72 86 |

DHANLAL BROTHERS DISTRIBUTORS
70, Princess Street, Mumbai – 400 002.
Phone : 201 70 27

S 273
G 509

**Visit us at :** www.navneet.com

**e-mail :** npil@navneet.com

© **All rights reserved. No part of this book may be copied, adopted, abridged or translated, stored in any retrieval system, computer system, photographic or other system or transmitted in any form by any means without a prior written permission of the copyright holders, M/s. Navneet Publications (India) Ltd.** ***Any breach will entail legal action and prosecution without further notice.***

*

**Dr. Dhiren Gala**

1st Floor, Abbas Building 'A',
Near Tilak Market, Jalbhai Lane,
Harkishandas Hospital Road,
Mumbai – 400 004.
Phone : 386 72 75

*

**Publishers :**

Navneet Publications (India) Ltd.,
Dantali, Gujarat.

*

**Printed by :**

Shreeji Offset
25/7, Manekchowk Mill Compound, Near Idgah Police Station,
Out of Dariyapur Darwaja, Ahmadabad. [12–12–2000 (10) : 5]

# PREFACE

**'Magnet therapy'** occupies a unique place among the non-medical modes of treatment widely tried by the people whose ailments are not cured by the known medical modes of treatment. It has, therefore, rightly raised hopes for those suffering from diseases that defy cure by prevalent medicines.

The advantages of Magnet therapy over the other modes of treatment are numerous. It is simple, effective and inexpensive, too. Moreover it has no harmful side effects.

We have tried to cover all important aspects of Magnet therapy in this book, carefully avoiding superfluous technical details.

The essential aim in bringing out a book of this nature is both to stimulate people to take necessary interest in the matter of their own health and to invite pointed attention of numerous medical practitioners to the benefits that could be derived from Magnet therapy.

As a matter of fact, medical practitioners can resort to this treatment as complementary to their own treatment.

Meticulous care has been taken in the production of this book but all the same, suggestions from the esteemed readers for its further improvements are solicited.

**–Authors**

# CONTENTS

# SECTION I : INTRODUCTION

## 1. THE THEORY OF MAGNET THERAPY

We are all well acquainted with Allopathy, the prevalent medical science. It is of great value in acute diseases and emergencies. Allopathic medicines can ameliorate acute symptoms and pain quite soon. Besides, advances in surgery have saved many a life. But the allopathic treatment for chronic illnesses leaves much to be desired. Basically, allopathic medicines give symptomatic relief. Long term use of such medicines is fraught with the danger of side-effects. New diseases, caused by medicines, are more difficult to treat, as compared to natural diseases.

Many a hope was raised when drugs like Thalidomide, corticosteroids and Penicillin were discovered. Big claims were made for the efficacy of these medicines. But people were disillusioned when they encountered grave side-effects of these medicines.

The awareness to such hazards of medicines has led people to resort to other modes of treatment like Magnet therapy, Acupressure, Acupuncture, Yoga therapy, Nature cure etc. These modes of treatment are simple and effective. At the same time,they are devoid of harmful side-effects. It is no wonder they are becoming more and more popular.

Amongst the great forces of nature, magnetism occupies a place of pride. The fact that natural magnetism influences all forms of life is supported by all physicists and biologists. Based on this principle, a new mode of treatment, which uses suitable artificial magnets as healing tools, has come into existence.

**[Side-effects of Thalidomide]**

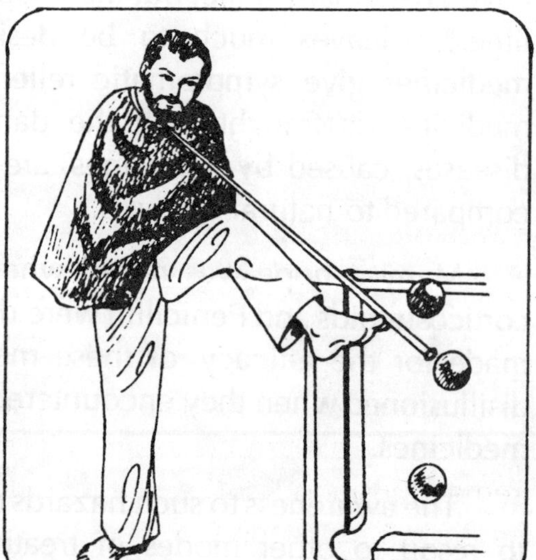

Earth itself is a huge magnet and possesses a magnetic field. All bodies in space, including the sun and the moon, have their own magnetic fields. Thus, man is constantly surrounded by and lives in a sea of magnetic waves and is influenced by them. It is, therefore, natural that health can be restored or maintained with the help of a controlled magnetic field emanating from artificial magnets.

In spite of the fact that each new day heralds the invention of new and sophisticated instruments to diagnose and treat diseases, the scene of health is no brighter than what it was a few years (or decades) ago. In fact, labouring to invent new drugs or new instruments is not the right approach to fight diseases. Man should strive to gain knowledge about the factors that undermine health and about the physiological forces acting inside the human body. With such knowledge, a disease can be prevented. Prevention is not only better than cure but cheaper too. In fact, giving a greater importance to the preventive aspect of treatment is the need of the day.

Magnet therapy is based upon the principle that disease is the result of an imbalance or inco-ordination between the various electromagnetic forces present inside the body. Magnet therapy strives to eliminate such inco-ordination and restore the natural balance of forces. Thus magnet therapy looks upon a human being as a whole unit. Its aim is not mere symptomatic relief or palliation of distress.

Magnets have been used in physics, industry and commerce since long. Their effects upon certain metals are also well-known. The knowledge that they can affect living beings is comparatively recent.

Magnet therapy is not only a science but an art, too. It has wide applications. Almost every disease can be treated with magnets. This therapy has a firm, scientific base. It has gained tremendous popularity and acceptance in countries like Japan, America, Russia and Germany. In our country, it is less known; but its message is spreading fast.

<u>Summary</u> :

1. Aware of the possible side-effects of modern drugs, people are now turning to Magnet therapy.
2. A disease is the result of imbalance between the various electromagnetic forces acting inside the body. Balance can be restored with artificial magnets and good health regained.
3. Magnet therapy is very popular in many advanced countries. In our country, too, it is spreading fast.

## 2. THE HISTORY OF MAGNET THERAPY

Ancient Aryans (Indians) knew about magnets and some of their properties. They believed that magnets not only attract iron but also possess mysterious and healing properties.

There are a few references in Atharva Veda (a sacred book) about the treatment of certain diseases with 'Sikta' and 'Ashman' which mean sand and stone respectively. These were used to control uterine bleeding and to induce sterility. Ordinary sand or stone cannot have such powers. Even today, ceramic magnets are manufactured from sand, clay and iron. Thus, one can assume that sand and stone, referred to in ancient texts, meant magnets.

Ancient Greeks, too, were acquainted with natural magnets. Renowned philosophers Aristotle, Plato and Homer have mentioned the properties of magnets in their works. The Roman poet Titus Carus has stated in his book 'The rarum natura' that a clip clinging to a natural magnet itself exhibits magnetic properties, i.e., attracts another clip. Thus, 'magnetism by induction' was known even at that time.

Laymen ascribed miraculous properties to magnets. Cleopatra, the beautiful daughter of Egyptian king Tolemi, always wore a small magnet on her forehead with a view to preserving her beauty and youthfulness. Thieves carried magnets with them, thinking that magnets would prevent them from being caught. A person would carry a magnet on his body to keep his beloved attracted to himself or to bring about a reunion with a lost dear one. It was also believed that certain submerged mountains in the North sea were magnets and forcibly pulled away nails from ships. Therefore, wooden nails came to be used in the manufacture of ships.

Thus, magnets found a place in the Vedas and other ancient texts. Some physicians knew about their healing properties. But

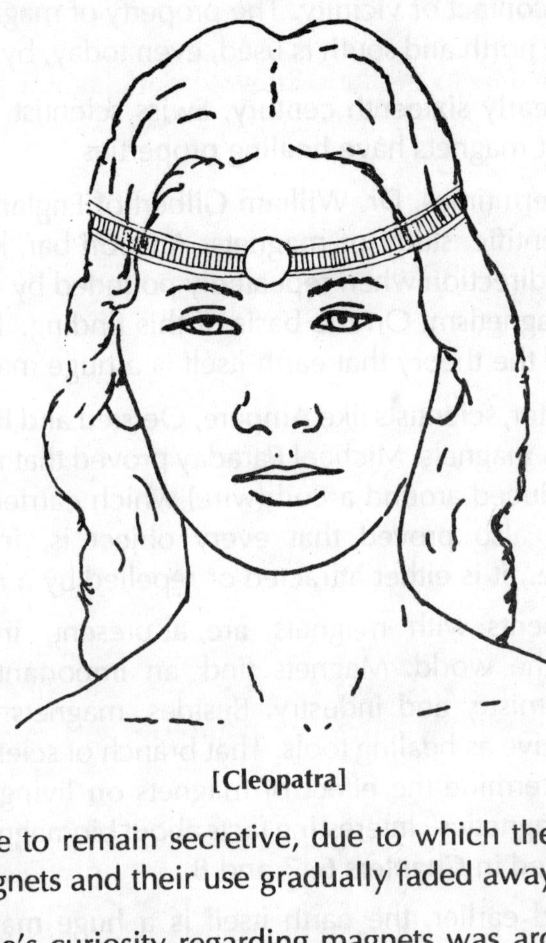

**[Cleopatra]**

they chose to remain secretive, due to which the knowledge about magnets and their use gradually faded away.

People's curiosity regarding magnets was aroused again, some 2500 years back. It is said that an iron rod carried by a shepherd named Magnetis got stuck to a stone and it was only with difficulty that he could detach it. The stone was, therefore, named 'a magnet'. According to another view, iron ore ($Fe_3O_4$) was found in abundance in a place called Magnesia. This iron ore had attracting properties. The term magnet was thus derived from Magnesia.

Till the end of the fifteenth century, people knew only of two properties of a magnet: (1) its ability to stabilise in the north-south direction if hung freely and (2) its ability to induce (though temporarily) magnetism in suitable substances which were in its contact or vicinity. The property of magnet to point towards the north and south is used, even today, by navigators.

In the early sixteenth century, Swiss scientist Paracelsus claimed that magnets have healing properties.

In modern times, Dr. William Gilbert of England laid the base of scientific study of magnets. An iron bar, kept in the north-south direction when repeatedly pounded by a hammer, develops magnetism. On the basis of this finding, Dr. Gilbert propounded the theory that earth itself is a huge magnet.

Thereafter, scientists like Ampere, Oersted and Biot experimented with magnets. Michael Faraday proved that a magnetic field is produced around a coil (wire) which carries electrical current. He also proved that every object is, in a sense, magnetic, i.e., it is either attracted or repelled by a magnet.

Experiments with magnets are, at present, in progress throughout the world. Magnets find an important place in physics, chemistry and industry. Besides, magnets have also proved effective as healing tools. That branch of science which strives to determine the effect of magnets on living beings is called 'Biomagnetics'. Interesting facts about biomagnetics have been presented in Chapters 6, 7 and 8.

As stated earlier, the earth itself is a huge magnet. The history of how the earth's magnetic field has affected life is both interesting and instructive. The nature of the earth's magnetic field, thousands of years ago, can be determined by atomic dating method after drilling holes into volcanoes. Such experiments have revealed that in the era when giant dinosaurs reigned supreme, the magnetic field of the earth was quite high. As the magnetic field decreased, the size of the animals too progressively decreased. In other words, the changes in the earth's magnetic field have considerably influenced all the living beings as to their size, type and intelligence.

Studies of different volcanoes on the earth indicate that the north and the south magnetic poles of the earth have, from time to time, changed places. At present, the earth's magnetic north pole is situated at its geographic south pole, whereas its magnetic south pole is located at its geographic north pole. This view is supported by all the physicists.

**Summary :**

1. There are references in Atharva Veda, the ancient text, that magnets can be used to bring about specific changes in the human body.
2. In ancient times, people ascribed mysterious properties to magnets.
3. Earth itself is a huge magnet. It should be clearly understood that the earth's magnetic south pole is situated at its geographical north pole and vice versa.
4. Experiments to determine the effects of magnets on vegetation, insects, animals and human beings are incessantly being performed. This field of science is termed 'Biomagnetics'.

# 3. MAGNETISM : AN IMPORTANT AND OMNIPRESENT FORCE

The most important forces of nature include gravity, radiation, the nuclear force and the electromagnetic force. Magnetism is a part of the electromagnetic force. Though many a thing about electromagnetism is still ill-understood, the fact remains that it is an extremely important force. Electromagnetic energy is propagated in the form of waves. These electromagnetic waves are all-pervading. In fact, electromagnetism is present in every thing, living or non-living.

Let us take the simple example of a hydrogen atom. The nucleus of the hydrogen atom consists of a proton which constantly spins around its own axis. This rotatory movement gives rise to a magnetic field. Thus, the proton acts as small magnet. Besides, the hydrogen atom has an extra-nuclear electron which not only rotates around its own axis but also revolves round the central proton. These actions of the electron also contribute to the magnetic field of the hydrogen atom.

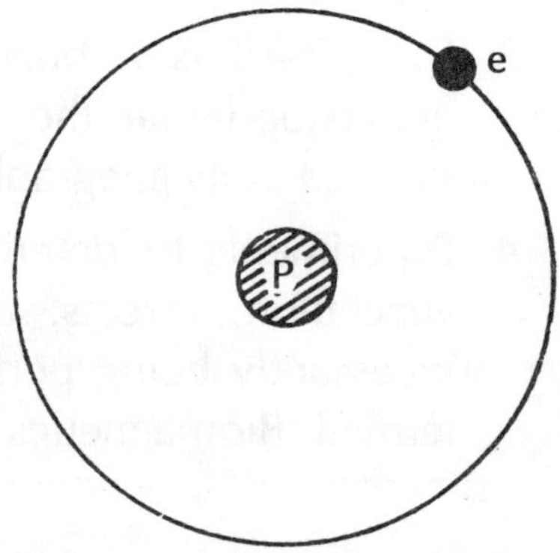

[ Fig. 3.1 : Hydrogen Atom ]

Thus, an atom is the smallest magnet existent. Since every substance is made up of atoms, electromagnetic waves are omnipresent and electromagnetism is an indivisible part of the universe. An universe devoid of electromagnetic waves cannot be imagined.

Magnetism is a fundamental force, which affects the whole universe. Magnetic waves emanate from the earth, the moon and the sun and influence the life on the earth.

**Earth : a huge natural magnet**

(1) A blacksmith's anvil, if placed in the north-south direction, develops magnetism.

(2) A vertical bar of iron gradually develops magnetic properties.

(3) If an iron bar is suspended in the north-south direction, its north end gradually develops into a magnetic north pole and the south end develops into a magnetic south pole.

(4) A freely suspended magnet always stabilises in the north south direction.

These facts are irrefutable proofs of the earth's magnetic field.

The magnetic field of the earth forms an envelope around the earth. This envelope is thousands of kilometres thick. Sputnik 3 and other satellites have confirmed the presence of earth's magnetic field even at the distance of 1,05,600 kilometres from the surface of the earth.

Many theories have been propounded to explain how the earth's magnetism originates. The two most accepted theories are as follows :

(1) The earth's magnetism originates because of the spinning of the earth about its own axis.

(2) The earth's magnetism originates because of the electricity generated by the charged ions (particles possessing electrical charges) present in the atmosphere, especially the ionosphere.

Beyond the ionosphere of the earth, there is a vast area full of dangerous radiations. This area or envelope is called the Van Allen belt. The earth's magnetic field effectively prevents these harmful radiations from reaching the earth's surface. Thus, this magnetic field serves a protective purpose for all living beings. Without this field, life would not have become possible. The same argument can be extended to state that diseases can be cured and health restored by using suitable magnets.

The earth's magnetic field is quite weak, measuring only about 0.5 gauss. But it is adequate to protect and sustain life.

Extensive studies enable scientists to assume that the magnetic poles of the earth have changed ends. During such a change, a time must have come when the earth's magnetic field must have plunged to zero. Probably, it was at this time that the giant dinosaurs and other animals met their doom. Only a few animals and plants with superlative resistance survived.

**It should be clear that the earth's magnetic north pole is situated at its geographic south pole and the magnetic south pole is situated at its geographic north pole. This has been established by extensive studies with the help of satellites. This fact should be kept in mind while determining or naming the poles of an unknown and unmarked magnet.**

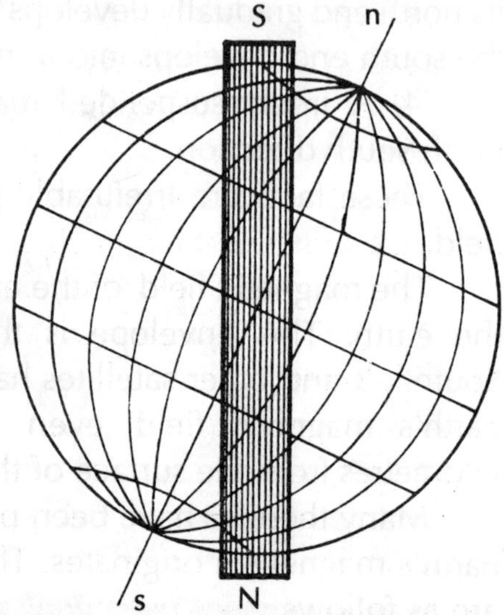


**[Fig. 3.2 : Earth – A Huge Magnet]**

S and N : Earth's magnetic south and north poles, respectively
s and n : Earth's geographical south and north poles, respectively

**The effect of earth's magnetic field on human life :** Baron Von Richenbach has shown through experiments that sensitive persons find discomfort and become agitated if made to lie down with their heads towards the south. However, their minds become relaxed and peaceful and they fall asleep when they lie down with their heads towards the north. They cannot sleep so soundly when lying down in any other direction. In short, when a person remains parallel to the earth's magnetic field, he can accomplish any work with least difficulty.

In his book 'Earth's Magnetic Field and Man', John Pierakos writes that certain crystals constantly undergo rhythmic changes in their shapes. The frequency of such changes or oscillations depends upon the crystal's position in relation to that of the earth, e.g., when the main edge of a quartz crystal faces the south, the crystal changes its shape nine times every minute. When the crystal faces, turn by turn, the west, the east and the north, its shape undergoes changes six times, fourteen times and four times a minute respectively. Thus, the crystal experiences least excitation when its main edge faces the north. Similarly, a person lying down with his head facing the north experiences relaxation and falls asleep.

Experiments have shown that when the head of a person lies towards the north, alpha, delta and theta waves dominate inside his brain. Consequently, the thinking process gradually slows down and the person experiences peace. Thus, the brain requires the cooling and peace-giving waves emanating at the geographic north pole of the earth (i.e., its magnetic south pole). If lying down in the north-south direction is not possible, a flat magnet can be kept under the pillow such that the cool south pole lies upward, i.e., faces the person's head.

**Magnetism in the universe :** The sun, too, is a huge magnet. Magnetic storms occurring on the sun affect the life on the earth. This has been dealt with in detail in Chapter 5.

The moon also is a magnet and affects the life on the earth. It is well-known that mad persons get excited on full-moon days. Our age-old custom of fasting on full-moon days and no-moon days has a scientific base.

All other bodies in space emit electromagnetic waves. Thus, the whole universe is laden with magnetism.

**Summary :**

1. Every object in this universe is a magnet. Every magnet has a magnetic field. Thus, we live in the midst of magnetic waves.
2. Earth is a huge magnet. The magnetic south pole of the earth is located at its geographical north pole and vice versa.
3. The sun and the moon are magnets. Their magnetic waves affect life on the earth.

# 4. LIFE : AN ELECTROMAGNETIC PHENOMENON

Science deals only with physical quantities, i.e., matter which can be seen or measured. It can very well describe the structure of our body, the numerous processes occurring in our body. But it can throw little light upon the force which keeps the body-processes going.

Dr. Bellokossy of Denewer describes life as 'an infinitely intelligent interaction of electromagnetic energies carried by chemical substances'. Without the driving force, the body would be non-functional, i.e., dead. We call this driving force, 'Prana'.

According to Dr. Alexei Gubko of the Ukrainian Institute of Psychology, every cell of our body is an electrical unit. Therefore, it possesses a magnetic field. Every organ of our body has a specific magnetic field, different from that of any other organ.

It is believed that the sources of the electromagnetic field of the human body are the sodium, potassium and chloride ions (charged particles) produced during the contraction of muscles or conduction of messages along the nerves. The magnetic substances present in the body are also thought to be the sources of body's electromagnetic field.

The condition of a body-part or an organ can be easily judged by measuring its magnetic field. For example, with the magneto-cardiogram, it can be easily determined whether the heart is healthy or not or whether there is some imminent danger to it. Similarly, with magneto-encephalogram and magnetomyogram, one can come to know about the state of health of the brain and muscles respectively. Such findings are more accurate as compared to an electro-encephalogram (EEG) or electro-myogram (EMG). At present, however, such facilities are not available in our country.

Every organ of our body has a specific oscillatory (or vibratory) frequency. In disease, this natural oscillatory frequency gets altered. In short, a disease is the result of the loss of (or a change in) the natural frequency of vibration. Symptoms or signs of the disease are the external manifestations of this derangement or disturbance. The causes for such derangement of natural vibratory frequencies have been discussed in Chapter 9. With suitable magnets, the natural vibratory frequency of the concerned cells or the organ can be restored and consequently health can be regained. Thus Magnet therapy strikes at the root of disease. It does not strive merely to palliate symptoms.

In his book 'Human Culture and Cure', Dr. Babbit states : 'The right side of our body possesses inhibitory or retarding electrical forces whereas the left side possesses stimulating or augmentative forces. When these opposing forces are well-balanced, health is maintained. Thus, according to Magnet therapy, health is a condition of the body, in which the magnetic fields of the various organs are in a state of perfect harmony'.

Dr. Barnwell and Dr. Brown of the North-Western University, U.S.A., after performing numerous experiments to determine the effects of magnetic field on living beings state that 'There now remains no reasonable doubt that all living organisms are extraordinarily sensitive to magnetic fields'.

**Summary :**

1. Life is an electromagnetic phenomenon.
2. The cells and organs of our body possess magnetism. They constantly undergo vibrations. If there is co-ordination and harmony between the vibrations of different organs, a person stays in good health. If due to some reason, the co-ordination is disturbed, disease ensues.
3. Suitable magnets restore the natural vibratory frequency of organs and re-establish co-ordination between them. Thus, disease disappears and health is regained.

## 5. THE BEARING OF THE EARTH'S MAGNETIC FIELD UPON LIVING BEINGS

Prominent researchers have detected a correlation between the magnetic storms taking place on the sun, the earth's magnetic field and the life on the earth.

Magnetic storms frequently occur on the sun. These storms are manifested as sun-spots and flares. According to the intensity and the number of sun-storms taking place, years have been classified as (1) high sun-spot year, (2) medium sun-spot year and (3) low sun-spot year.

The solar magnetic storms affect the earth's magnetic field. They bring about fluctuations in its strength. Such fluctuations or oscillations of the earth's magnetic field adversely affect the life on the earth. The body as well as the mind of creatures with a low vitality (resistance power) are more likely to be affected. It is a proven fact that the incidence of physical and mental illnesses increases during a high sun-spot year.

Let us consider the findings of some studies undertaken in our country. To determine the effects of the intensity of sun-storms upon the incidence of heart-disease, data was collected from hospitals in Hyderabad and Secunderabad for the years 1972 (medium sun-spot year), 1975 (low sun-spot year) and 1978 (high sun-spot year). It was quite clear that the incidence of heart-disease was much greater in high sun-spot year.

Data was also obtained from the traffic police department and the Indian air force to determine the number of road and air accidents that occurred, solely due to the driver's mistake, during the period 1970 – '74. It was evident from the figures that the incidence of accidents was much higher during high sun-spot years (i.e., 1970 and 1974).

Thus, it can be said that the fluctuations or oscillations in the earth's magnetic field caused by magnetic storms on the sun prove detrimental to health, especially of those living beings, who have a low resistance power.

The earth's magnetic field also undergoes changes on a full-moon day, a no-moon day or during a cyclone. At such times human beings are known to be affected, mentally as well as physically.

It is an age-old custom in India to compel a pregnant woman to take complete rest during an eclipse. The so-called 'scientific' persons ridicule such customs. But the basis behind such a custom can now readily be understood. The fluctuations in the earth's magnetic field during an eclipse adversely affect the pregnant woman's mind. If she does not take due care during such time, an untoward incident may occur.

Scientific studies have shown that fishes which normally live in shallow waters migrate into deep waters during sun-storms or cyclones.

Circumstances or changes simulating a magnetic storm, when produced in a laboratory, have exactly similar effects on experimental animals. All those animals who have a low vitality suffer from illnesses of cardio-vascular or nervous systems.

**Summary :**

1. Magnetic storms on the sun have undesirable effects on living beings of the earth. At such times, a disorder of the heart, circulatory system or the nervous system is likely to occur.
2. Efforts are being made to determine the exact nature of the biochemical changes that take place inside the body during fluctuations of earth's magnetic field.
3. Once the precise nature of changes becomes known, rational measures to dodge illnesses can be contemplated.

# 6. BIOMAGNETICS 1 : THE EFFECTS OF MAGNETISM ON PLANT LIFE

Experiments to determine the effects of the magnetic field on life were initially performed on lower forms of life like seeds and plants.

Earth itself is a huge magnet, with its south pole situated at the geographic north pole and the north pole situated at the geographic south pole. Though its strength is only 0.5 gauss, its presence is extremely vital for the existence of all living beings, since it serves a great protective function.

In an experiment, some seeds were taken. They were sown in such a way that their 'eyes' (micropyles) faced all possible directions. Later, it was seen that all those seeds, whose eyes had faced the south, germinated much faster than the rest. This experiment was repeated again and again taking seeds of different varieties. The results obtained were the same every time. This was an early proof of the fact that the earth's magnetic field affects life.

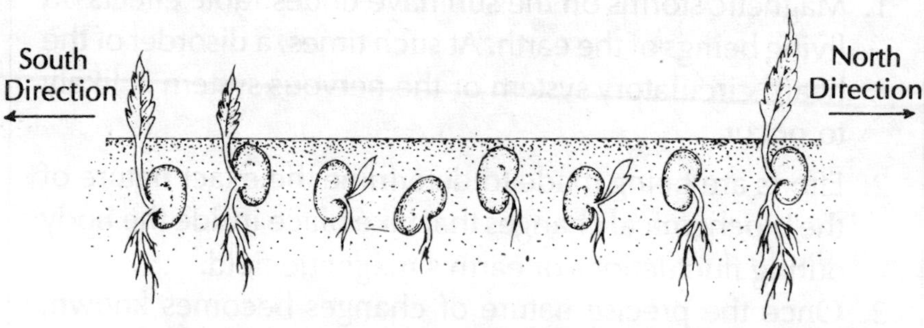


**[Fig. 6.1 : Effects of Earth's Magnetic Field on Germination of Seeds]**

Another experiment was performed on raddish seeds Before sowing them, some seeds were treated for a few hours with the north pole of a powerful magnet. Some others were treated with the south pole of a powerful magnet. These were then sown in separate pots. A third group of 'untreated' seeds was sown in another pot. This was the 'control' group. It was seen that the growth rate of seeds treated with magnets for more than four hours was different from that of untreated or control seeds. Seeds treated with the north pole of the magnet germinated and grew faster than the control seeds. On the other hand, seeds treated with the south pole lagged behind the control seeds in development.

**Thus the north pole of a magnet was found to be stimulating or augmentative, whereas the south pole turned out to be inhibitive to growth.**

The same experiment, conducted on tomato seeds, produced similar results. Tomato seeds influenced with the north pole germinated faster. Their plants grew taller and bore larger tomatoes. These plants extracted more carbon dioxide from the atmosphere and released more oxygen than the control plants. Their roots penetrated deeper into the soil and were larger in dimensions. The seeds treated with the south pole grew slowly, gave rise to shorter plants and produced smaller tomatoes. These tomatoes, however, had less amount of acids, were sweeter and hence proved congenial even to persons with gastric hyperacidity.

In Puerto Rico, experiments with magnets have been conducted on farms and orchards. Whole farms are constantly influenced by strong magnetic fields. This has led to a steep rise in the yield of these farms. The plants and trees in such farms are more fertile, bear heavy fruit and can withstand adverse weather conditions very easily.

Sweet potatoes, influenced with magnets, have been found to possess more sugar. Groundnut seeds and plants, when influenced with magnets, produce groundnuts that have high protein and oil-contents. In short, magnetisation not only increases the yield but improves the nutritive value of vegetables, fruits and cereals.

Another experiment has revealed that magnets also affect the ripening of fruits. Fruits influenced by the north pole of a magnet ripen faster than untreated (control) fruits. If not removed from the magnetic influence, they get over-ripe and begin to rot. On the other hand, fruits influenced by a south pole ripen slowly and hence remain fresh for a longer time.

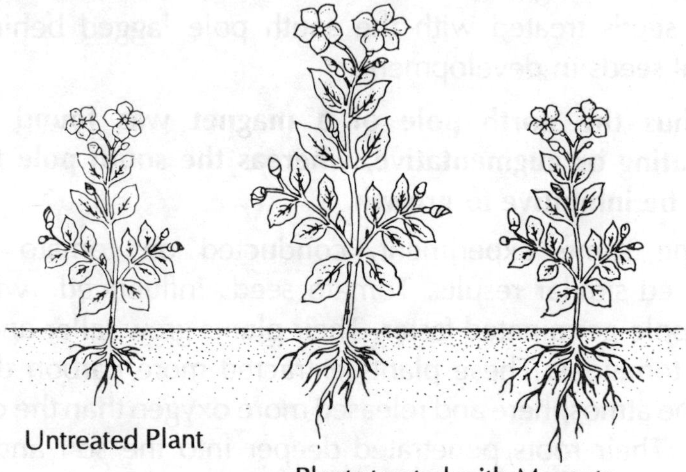


**[Fig. 6.2 : Effects of Magnetic Field on Plant-growth]**

Similar encouraging results are obtained by using magnetised water, too. Farms and orchards, irrigated with magnetised water, give a much greater yield. Plants and trees in such farms have been found to be much stronger and can withstand strong winds or frost quite easily.

**Summary :**

1. Magnets affect plant-growth.
2. Seeds stimulated with the north pole of a magnet germinate earlier and grow into taller plants with heavy foliage. Seeds stimulated with the south pole germinate later than usual, show sluggish development and grow into shorter plants with lesser foliage.
3. Plants can be favourably influenced by irrigating them with 'magnetised water'. Such plants can easily withstand adverse weather.

# 7. BIOMAGNETICS 2 : THE EFFECTS OF MAGNETISM ON BIRDS AND ANIMALS

The effects of the magnetic field on plant life were known. It was essential to determine its effects on animals as well.

Russians were the first to initiate such research. They used the north and the south poles simultaneously. Dr. Komarov of 'The Institute of General Genetics' has performed many experiments on insects and animals. Dr. Komarov succeeded in almost doubling the life of the common housefly by feeding it with 'magnetised' sugar. Encouraged with such a result, Dr. Komarov and his co-workers established the National Committee on prolongation of human life. This committee performs experiments with magnets on human volunteers. The metabolic and biochemical changes occurring in the human body, following an exposure to the magnetic field, are being assessed. **The committee is hopeful that magnetic treatment will enable scientists to prolong human life to 400 years !**

After numerous experiments, Dr. Harold Alexander of America has concluded that a specific exposure of rats to a magnetic field increases their life-span by about 45 per cent.

Russian scientists, too, have been able to prolong the life of mice with magnets. An experimental female mouse surprised scientists by giving birth to three small mice at the old age of four years. Normally, mice do not reproduce after the age of three years.

Experiments on animals with the magnetic field are in progress in England and Puerto Rico, too. In an experiment, animals with severe radioactive burns were treated with magnets. They beat all odds and survived. Other animals, not treated with magnets, died within hours of getting burns. This discovery holds great prospects for human beings. It is a known fact that leakages from atomic plants and reactors frequently occur. Such a leakage creates grave hazards for life. In such circumstances (or during a nuclear war), magnets may prevent total destruction of the human race and prevent congenital abnormalities and disabilities in future generations.

Experiments with magnets have also been performed on cows. Experimental cows were not only exposed to a magnetic field but also fed with magnetised food and water. These cows gave much more milk than other normal cows.

In another experiment, mice were exposed to a strong magnetic field for a few hours. Their urines were analysed for sodium and potassium contents. It was evident that the sodium-content as well as the potassium content of the urine had increased (sodium from 2.34 mg% to 4.29 mg% and potassium from 9.14 mg% to 14.59 mg%). This meant that magnets had stimulated the adrenal glands to secrete more aldosterone. This was a decisive proof that magnets can influence the endocrine glands of the body.

It should be noted that in all the above experiments, both north and south poles were used together. In the year 1936, it was discovered by Dr. Albert Roy Davis of America that the north and the south poles of a magnet have different properties and produce different effects on animals. Dr. Davis had been experimenting on earthworms for some time. Once, two boxes containing earthworms were inadvertently placed in contact with a U-shaped magnet. The north pole of the magnet remained in contact with one box and the south pole with the other.

A few hours later, when Dr. Davis' attention was drawn towards the boxes, he was amazed. The earthworms in the vicinity of the north pole had eaten away a part of the cardboard box and had escaped out. But the earthworms in the vicinity of the south pole were lying inactive inside the box. To ascertain that this effect had been produced by the magnet, Dr. Davis divided the 'south pole' earthworms into three groups. Each group was packed into a separate box, each having similar environment. Thereafter, one box was kept in contact with the north pole, the second with the south pole and the third was kept far away from the magnet. On examination some hours later, it was found that the earthworms influenced by the north pole had become active and aggressive and had eaten their way out of the box. They were seen to be larger in size because they had consumed more food. Besides, they had laid more eggs inside the box, some of which had even been hatched. The earthworms influenced with the south pole were seen to be lazy and inactive. The earthworms not influenced with any magnet showed normal development and activity.

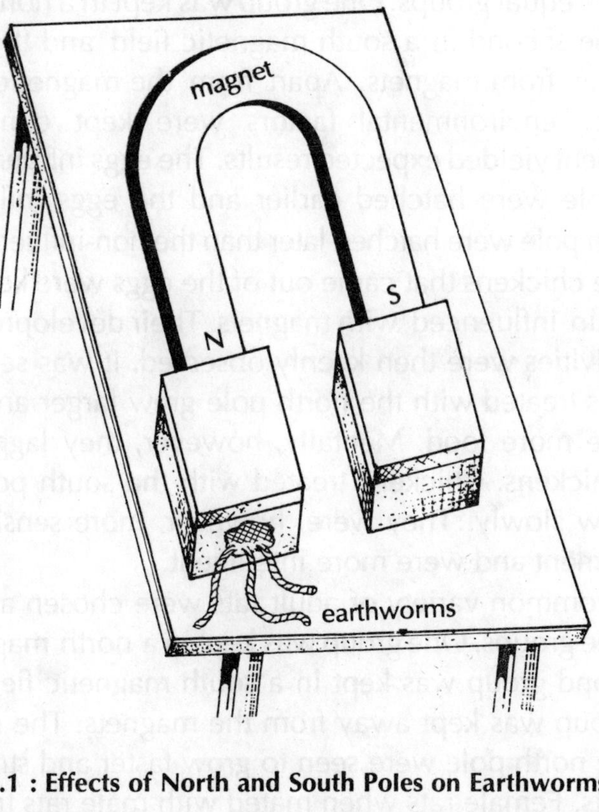


**[Fig. 7.1 : Effects of North and South Poles on Earthworms]**

The experiment was repeated using magnets of different strengths. It was seen that the activity and strength of the earthworms was directly proportional to the strength of the magnets used.

To determine whether the magnets were also influencing the body-chemistry, the urine of each group of earthworms was analysed. The urine of earthworms influenced with the north pole had greater amounts of urea, hormones and fat, as compared to those of the other two groups.

It was found that magnets with strengths of 2000 to 4500 gauss were the most effective in producing results. 100 gauss was the lowest power of magnets which could elicit a response.

These results encouraged scientists to perform more experiments.

For an experiment, 24 eggs were taken. They were divided into three equal groups. One group was kept in a north magnetic field, the second in a south magnetic field and the third was kept away from magnets. Apart from the magnetic influence, all other environmental factors were kept constant. This experiment yielded expected results. The eggs influenced by the north pole were hatched earlier and the eggs influenced by the south pole were hatched later than the non-influenced eggs.

The chickens that came out of the eggs were kept in cages and again influenced with magnets. Their development, habits and activities were then keenly observed. It was seen that the chickens treated with the north pole grew larger and stronger. They ate more food. Mentally, however, they lagged behind other chickens. Chickens treated with the south pole are less and grew slowly. They were, however, more sensitive to the environment and were more intelligent.

A common variety of adult rats were chosen and divided into three groups. One group was kept in a north magnetic field, the second group was kept in a south magnetic field and the third group was kept away from the magnets. The rats treated with the north pole were seen to grow faster and stronger than other rats. Female rats when mated with male rats treated with magnets conceived more easily and gave birth to more babies. Magnets, in general, were seen to prolong the reproductive age of the rats.

A very important experiment was conducted on a variety of animals like rats, rabbits, guinea pigs, cats and dogs. Cancer cells were implanted into the bodies of these animals and due care was taken to ensure that these cancer cells were not rejected by their bodies. Thereafter, these animals were kept in strong magnetic fields. This experiment revealed that the south pole succeeded in arresting the growth of cancer in almost 90 per cent animals. On the other hand, the north pole stimulated the cancerous tissue to grow rapidly, thereby worsening the condition. Magnets were kept in contact with the cancer site for 45 minutes, three times a day.

Dr. Shiro Saito of the Jikei Medical College, Japan has also succeeded in arresting cancer in animals. He is hopeful that magnets will also cure cancer in human beings. He is doing extensive research to achieve such results. Such a discovery will prove a great boon to mankind because the prevalent treatment for cancer (medicines, radiation and surgery) leaves much to be desired.

**Summary :**

1. Magnets affect higher forms of life like insects and animals, as well.
2. House-flies and rats fed with magnetised food live longer. Dr. Komarov of Russia is hopeful that magnets will enable a man to live for 400 years.
3. Animals when kept in a magnetic field are not harmed even when bombarded with dangerous radiation. Scientists are hopeful that magnets will save human beings too, when a nuclear war breaks out.
4. Cows treated with magnets or fed with magnetised fodder yield more milk.
5. Rats treated with magnets stay young for a longer time and retain their reproductive powers.
6. The north pole and the south pole of a magnet have been found to possess opposing properties.
7. With the south pole of a strong magnet, cancer in rats was arrested or cured.

# 8. BIOMAGNETICS 3 : THE EFFECTS OF MAGNETISM ON MANKIND

Experiments with magnets on plants and animals were quite successful. It now remained to be seen whether magnets were beneficial to mankind as well.

Though human beings and certain higher animals (especially mammals) have anatomical and physiological similarities, there is one vital difference, that of intelligence and thinking power. Every person thinks individually. Animals, however, display collective consciousness. Man's actions arise from his intelligence. Most of the animal's actions arise instinctively. Man today lives a hectic life and is burdened with unprecedented mental tension. It is now universally agreed that the mind affects the physique, i.e., most diseases are psychosomatic. Every mode of treatment is first tried on animals. After it proves successful and harmless, it can be tried on human beings. In this context, two questions arose in scientists' minds :

(1) Can the various chemicals, hormones and enzymes inside the human body be influenced by magnets ? Can the functioning of the various systems of the body be altered by the use of magnets ?

(2) Can such changes be controlled as per one's will ?

A lot of research has been done to get answers to the above questions.

The results of the numerous experiments conducted at the Delawar Laboratories, Oxford, England have been presented in a book 'Biomagnetism'. The scientists of the Delawar Laboratories have devised an instrument called electronic reflexograph to detect and measure the minute changes that occur inside the body, following exposure to a magnetic field. This electronic reflexograph is more sensitive and accurate than electrocardiograph and sphygmomanometer which are currently used to measure the electrical impulses of the heart and blood pressure, respectively.

In an experiment, a number of body-parts of experimental subjects were simultaneously stimulated by suitable magnets. The electronic reflexograph was used to determine the changes in body-temperature, the oxygen-uptake by body-cells, the blood sugar level and the blood-cell count. It was evident that all the above entities were definitely affected by magnets.

The effects of the magnetic field upon the blood-cholesterol level, white cell count and blood pressure have been described below.

**Decrease in the blood-cholesterol level :** It is a known fact that when the level of cholesterol in the blood is high, the former gets deposited on the inner surface of blood vessels, rendering them narrow, hard and brittle. Such condition of blood vessels is termed 'atherosclerosis'. With the passage of time, atherosclerosis invariably leads to heart disease.

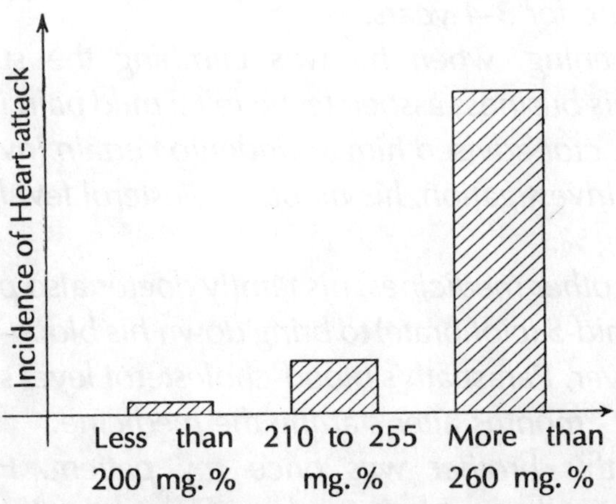


**[Fig. 8.1 : Serum Cholesterol Level and Heart-attack]**

In an experiment, 11 subjects were chosen for magnetic treatment. They were treated for 30 minutes, twice a week. All other factors (food, medicines, etc.) were kept unchanged. The results obtained after a month have been tabulated below :

**Blood Cholesterol Level in mg %**

| Person | Before treatment | After treatment | Reduction |
|---|---|---|---|
| AB | 277 | 215 | 62 |
| CD | 213 | 153 | 57 |
| EF | 294 | 243 | 51 |
| GH | 267 | 246 | 21 |
| IJ | 272 | 191 | 81 |
| KL | 273 | 227 | 46 |
| MN | 254 | 227 | 27 |
| OP | 282 | 251 | 31 |
| QR | 284 | 251 | 33 |
| ST | 303 | 238 | 65 |
| UV | 263 | 253 | 10 |

**Author's experience :** *Parasnath Jain, a large-scale manufacturer of synthetic yarn at Bhiwandi, near Mumbai, had high blood pressure for 3-4 years.*

*One evening, when he was climbing the stairs of the building of his business associate, he felt a mild pain in his chest. His family doctor advised him to undergo certain investigations. In one such investigation, his blood cholesterol level was found to be 293 mg %.*

*Besides other medicines, his family doctor also prescribed a drug, Actromid-S (clofibrate) to bring down his blood-cholesterol level. However, Parasnath's blood-cholesterol level still stood at 290 mg %, $1\frac{1}{2}$ months after starting the medicine.*

*Parasnath's brother was once my patient. He brought Parasnath to me. I gave him two pairs of magnets (one of medium power and the other of high power) and explained to him the method of using those magnets at home.*

*One month later, when Parasnath got his blood examined, the cholesterol level had fallen to 219 mg %.*

**A decrease in white blood-cell count :** In many diseases, especially infectious diseases, the number of white corpuscles in the blood increases. When the disease is controlled or cured, the white blood-cell count decreases to the normal number again. Thus, when the number of white cells decreases from the elevated value to the normal value, one can say that health has been regained.

In an experiment, 10 persons suffering from infectious diseases were treated with magnets. The treatment comprised of 2 sessions per week, each of 30 minutes' duration. At the end of two weeks, the disease was under control and the white blood-cell count had been normalised, as shown below :

**W.B.C. count per cubic mm of blood**

| Person | Before treatment | After treatment | Reduction |
|---|---|---|---|
| AB | 17600 | 9800 | 7800 |
| CD | 25300 | 10500 | 17800 |
| EF | 15700 | 10600 | 5100 |
| GH | 16700 | 9000 | 7700 |
| IJ | 15700 | 9500 | 6200 |
| KL | 16300 | 9700 | 6600 |
| MN | 16500 | 10500 | 6000 |
| OP | 15800 | 7500 | 8300 |
| QR | 24400 | 10500 | 13900 |
| ST | 24900 | 11500 | 13400 |

**A decrease in blood pressure :** In an experiment, several persons with high blood pressure were treated with magnets. Treatment comprised of 20 minute sessions, twice a week. Blood pressure was measured before and after each session. Every time a reduction of 5-10 mm Hg was recorded. The reduction per treatment was not very significant. But it was cumulative. After 2 months of treatment, the blood pressure of almost 60 per cent of subjects had dropped significantly.

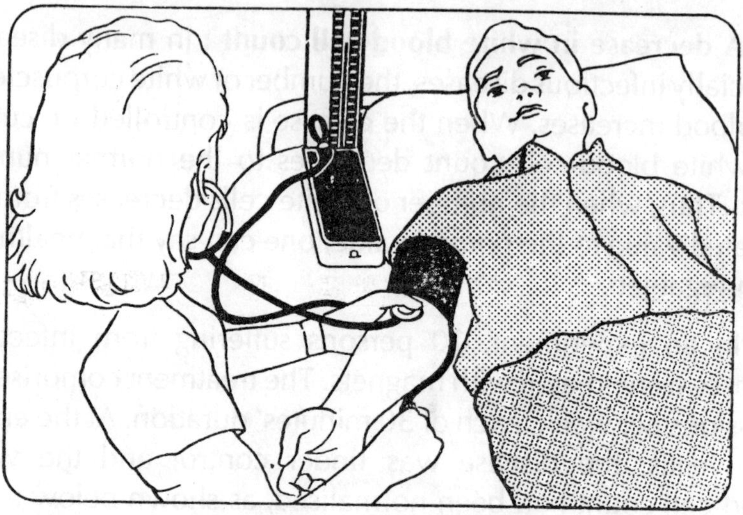

**[Fig. 8.2 : Measurement of B.P.]**

**Author's experience :** *Mr. Asumal Mirchandani, a resident of Chembur, Mumbai and a dealer in electronic goods at Lamington Road, had high blood pressure for a few months.*

*This disorder had been diagnosed accidentally. Asumal had visited his family physician for a urinary problem when, during routine examination, his blood pressure was found to be 190/135. He was prescribed a medicine for blood pressure. This medicine brought down his blood pressure to normal values. The treatment was continued regularly for about two months. Thereafter, Asumal left for a business tour to Singapore, where he could not take medicines regularly. When he returned, his blood pressure had rocketed to 210/140.*

*Asumal had heard and read about Magnet therapy and its efficacy in the treatment of blood pressure. He came to me. At that time, his blood pressure stood at 200/135.*

*Asumal expressed his inability to come to me regularly for treatment. Hence I gave him a magnetic belt to be continuously worn on the right wrist, a small magnet to be used below the right ear and a pair of high power magnets to prepare magnetised water. I gave him instructions regarding treatment and asked him to visit me every fortnight.*

*With the magnetic treatment, Asumal's blood pressure came*

*down gradually. Since the last few months, it has remained under control and steady at 150/100.*

The red blood corpuscles are also called erythrocytes. If a test-tube containing blood is revolved rapidly (centrifuged), the red blood-cells gradually settle down. The rate at which the red blood-cells get precipitated is called the 'erythrocyte sedimentation rate' or simply ESR. In good health the ESR is 0 to 10 mm per hour. In disease, the ESR rises. On eradication of the disease, the ESR comes down to reach normal values.

In an experiment, 100 subjects suffering from infectious diseases were treated with magnets. In all cases, as the disease came under control, the ESR values, too, normalised.

**Author's experience :** *One morning, Mr. Ashok Joshi came to see me. His mother Mrs. Niranjanabahen had been suffering from fever since last three weeks, due to which she was fast losing weight. There was no other symptom except the rise in temperature.*

*As per the advice of two leading physicians, Mr. Joshi had admitted his mother to a well-known hospital. In spite of numerous investigations, the cause of fever could not be ascertained. Doctors called this condition 'Pyrexia of unknown origin'. I visited Mrs. Niranjanabahen. Her condition was pitiable. It was not possible to methodically treat Niranjanabahen with magnets in the hospital. The only thing I could do was to advise Mr. joshi to give his mother magnetised water to drink, instead of plain water.*

*Four days later, Mrs. Niranjanabahen was discharged from the hospital. Thereafter, a full-fledged treatment with magnets was commenced. The treatment comprised of (1) keeping powerful magnets in contact with her palms and soles for 15 minutes, twice daily and (2) keeping small magnets in continuous contact (with the help of sticking plaster) of certain specific points on her body.*

*On the third day after starting Magnet therapy, Niranjanabahen showed first signs of improvement. Her temperature came down slightly and she expressed desire to eat something. Thereafter, the temperature continued to drop gradually and at the end of a week, it had become normal.*

*Niranjanabahen's ESR which was 60 mm per hour during her illness had now dropped to a normal 9 mm per hour.*

The results of the experiments with magnets opened up new avenues for fresh research and raised hopes for the cure of such diseases which are difficult to cure or are incurable with prevalent modes of treatment.

Physicians have used magnets to hasten wound-healing. When magnets are used, a lesser number of fibroblasts are needed to effect healing. Due to this decrease in fibrosis, very faint scars, if any, are left behind.

**Author's experience :** *A cyclist by hobby, Sneha Patkar once met with a minor accident. Her forehead crashed against a sharp stone lying on the road and a deep wound resulted.*

*When Sneha came to me, it was evident from her expression that the wound was causing acute pain. But Sneha said that she was more worried about developing an ugly scar on the forehead. I consoled her and asked her to apply the south pole of a 'medium-power' magnet to the wound-area for 20–30 minutes, three times a day.*

*This treatment not only brought about an early recovery but also ascertained that only a very faint scar was left behind.*

**Cancer research :** After eighteen long years of incessant research, 'Biomagnetic Research Foundation' of Chicago has claimed that a strong magnetic field can arrest the growth of cancer.

It has already been discussed earlier that cancer-cells transplanted into the bodies of rats could not develop if the animals were treated with magnets. Biomagnetic Research Foundation has experimented with magnets on natural cancer in human beings and has obtained promising results. There are numerous varieties of cancer and new varieties are constantly springing up. So, to say that all forms of cancer yield to Magnet therapy would be an exaggeration. But all cancer patients who have volunteered to give Magnet therapy a try have been benefited.

Dr. E. K. Maclean, a gynaecologist from New York, has used electromagnets to treat cancer. He accepts only such patients for magnetic treatment, who have been discarded by orthodox practitioners as hopeless. Yet Dr. Maclean has obtained encouraging results. According to Dr. Maclean's experience, magnets not only succeed in arresting the growth of cancer but many a time yield unexpected benefits like restoration of black colour to graying hair. Dr. Maclean claims that **'Cancer can't exist in a strong magnetic field !'**

**Fracture research :** 5 per cent of fractures, due to one reason or the other, fail to unite in spite of vigorous treatment including plaster, fastening with nails and screws and total rest.

In 1950, two Japanese orthopaedic surgeons demonstrated that if the fracture-site is stimulated, for a fixed duration of the day, with weak electrical current natural healing is hastened. Some years later, Dr. Brite of Pensylvania started using electro-magnetic impulses to expedite fracture-healing in his hospital. Since then, he has used this method successfully on hundreds of patients. In one case, a patient of non-union of a fracture, who was shunted from one hospital to the other for 10 years without success, was finally cured within six months by Dr. Brite.

**Author's experience :** *Mr. Vithaldas Gandhi suffered from fractured thigh bone following a scooter accident.*

*In spite of the best possible treatment including a plaster, for four months and a half, the fractured bone failed to unite. Doctors were worried. They were unable to prognose whether the fracture would heal or not.*

*Vithaldas' daugher-in-law had previously taken my treatment for her obesity. She knew that I was keenly interested in Magnet therapy. She came to me and casually inquired if Magnet therapy could help her father-in-law.*

*I said that Magnet therapy was definitely worth giving a try. I gave her a pair of strong magnets, which were to be applied to the fractured site for 45-60 minutes, three times a day. Besides, the same magnets were to be used to magnetise water. Such magnetised water was to be taken by the patient 3-4 times a day.*

*One and a half months later, Vithaldas himself came to me, with the support of a stick. The absence of plaster on his leg was self-explanatory. Vithaldas said that the plaster had been removed only two days back. He readily agreed to the fact that magnets had played a stellar role in effecting union of the broken bone-ends.*

Considering that magnets stimulate the production and development of new bone-cells, Magnet therapy may also prove to be of value in rarefaction of bones (osteoporosis).

**Research pertaining to the nervous system** : The ability of the magnets to stimulate the production and development of new cells has many implications.

When peripheral nerves are accidentally severed or cut, complete regeneration usually takes place and active function of the concerned body-part is restored. But cells of the spinal cord and the brain do not regenerate, once destroyed.

Experiments with magnets have, however, pointed to new possibilities. Some researchers performed experiments on animals. They deliberately severed the spinal cords of experimental animals. Thereafter, they interposed 'embryonic peripheral nerve tissue' between the opposing ends of the spinal cord and exposed that part continuously to a strong magnetic field. It was found that new cells grew in the spinal cord and successfully bridged the gap (formed due to experimental cutting). Thus the belief that spinal cells can never regenerate was belied.

This discovery has raised great hopes for persons suffering from paralysis of lower limbs, following an injury to the spinal cord. Scientists believe that even if 10 per cent of spinal cells can be revived, paralysis can be reversed and the person can be made to walk. In fact, scientists have succeeded in restoring the swimming ability of certain marine animals, whose spinal cord was experimentally severed.

This discovery also promises new hope to heart patients. After a heart-attack, a part of the heart is rendered dead. The heart muscles are of a special type, which cannot regenerate, once destroyed. But scientists have predicted regeneration of heart muscles too, with Magnet therapy. Of course, at present, this is only a dream; but it is based on a solid scientific foundation.

**Research on rheumatism and muscle pain :** Japanese scientists believe that when an organ of the body is diseased, its condition is reflected at (or relayed to) specific points on the skin, through autonomic nervous system. These points on the skin become tender and painful. Scientists call these points 'tsubos'.

Any person acquainted with Acupuncture or Acupressure will readily understand or appreciate the notion of tsubos. In Acupuncture, these tsubos are punctured with fine needles, whereby electrical impulses arise. These electrical impulses travel along the autonomic nerves to the diseased organ and effect a cure. It has been found that tsubos are also useful for application of magnets.

In rheumatoid arthritis, a number of tender and sensitive points are detected around the affected joints. A good amount of relief is obtained when these points are continuously stimulated with the north pole of small magnets. In cervical spondylosis, frozen shoulder, fibrositis and muscle-strain, too, tender points should be located and treated with magnets. Such treatment has effected a speedy cure in almost 60 per cent of patients, at leading centres all over the world.

**Author's experience :** *Mrs. Sumitrabahen Shroff, residing in Bhoiwada,* Mumbai *had suffered from pain and severe stiffness in the left shoulder for two and a half months. Even a slight effort to move the left arm caused acute pain in the shoulder. The condition had been diagnosed as 'Frozen shoulder'. Mrs. Shroff had tried analgesic (pain-killer) drugs, hot fomentation and massage, without any success. Besides, Mrs. Shroff also suffered from chronic backache.*

*In spite of the fact that she had to look after a big family, Mrs. Shroff agreed to come to me on every alternate day for Magnet therapy. I prescribed a magnetic waist belt for her backache, treatment with strong magnets for the shoulder joint and continuous treatment of specific pain-relieving points with small magnets.*

*With this treatment, Mrs. Shroff was relieved of her shoulder pain and backache in a short period of one month.*

Dr. Albert Roy Davis of America has used magnets with great success in many diseases.

The south pole of a strong magnet, when applied to the affected joint for 30-40 minutes, twice a day, proves quite effective in osteoarthritis. Osteoarthritis is characterised by growth of new, undesirable bone tissue along the periphery of bone ends. Such bony protuberances are called osteophytes. Following treatment with magnets, osteophytes get dissolved. This can be readily seen in radiographs.

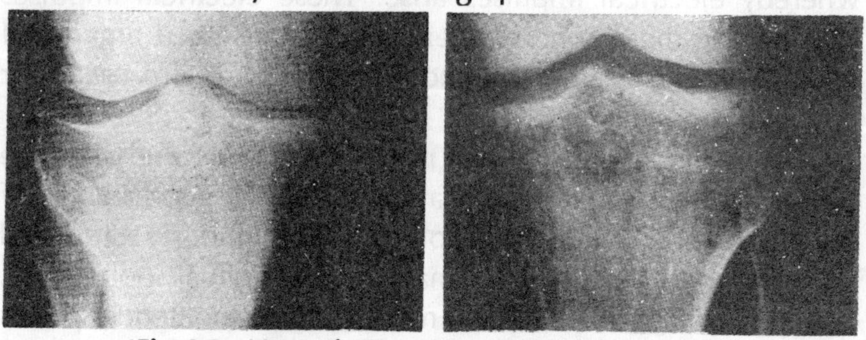

**[Fig. 8.3 : Magnetic Treatment of Osteoarthritis]**

Since the south pole is cool and relaxing it lessens inflammation (swelling) and relieves pain. This property is useful for the treatment of joint and muscle pain. Toothache, too, can be relieved by using the south pole of a strong magnet.

**Author's experience :** *Harendra Khurana, who used to come to me daily for eye-treatment, did not turn up for two days. On the third morning, he phoned me to say that acute toothache had compelled him to stay at home. I advised him to come to me.*

*When he visited me, his toothache was still there. A slight swelling was evident on his right cheek.*

*A single treatment session of half an hour with the south pole of a strong magnet effected a 75 per cent cure. Two more such sessions of treatments, during the next two days, resulted into a complete cure.*

The south pole is also useful for stopping loss of blood through wounds. During the second world war, Russian doctors used magnets to treat injured soldiers with great success.

Diabetes is the result of the deficiency of a hormone insulin, which is produced by the pancreas. In the adult variety of diabetes, if the stimulating and 'hot' north pole of a strong magnet is placed adjacent to the pancreas, the later produces more insulin and the blood sugar level can be effectively controlled. This can be proved by analysing blood before and after a treatment session.

**Author's experience :** *52-year old Mr. Kishorchandra Zaveri had diabetes for 3 years. He was taking a medicine (Diabinese–350 mg) to control the disease. However, he frequently had to face side-effects of this medicine, which included nausea and diarrhoea. Moreover, about an year back, the medicine had also caused jaundice. But Mr. Zaveri, fearing worse consequences of high blood sugar, could not even think of going without the medicine.*

*He agreed to come to me for magnetic treatment. On the sixth day after commencing Magnet therapy, he phoned me to say he was feeling giddy and weak. He also said that he was sweating profusely and was feeling a strange sensation in his stomach. It was quite evident that these were symptoms of hypoglycemia (abnormally low blood sugar). I advised him to take a sweet drink, which relieved the symptoms.*

*When Mr. Zaveri came to me, the next morning, he looked quite normal and healthy. But in the evening, symptoms of hypoglycemia recurred with a greater acuteness. This was a clear indication for slightly reducing the dosage of Diabinese.*

*Thereafter, symptom of hypoglycemia kept on recurring every 3-4 days. We went on decreasing the medicine dosage gradually. Of course, urine analysis was done every day to ensure that sugar was not escaping. Finally, when the medicine dosage was reduced to 100 mg, symptoms of hypoglycemia disappeared and did not recur.*

*For last seven months, Mr. Zaveri has been taking Magnet therapy at his own home. His diabetes is under complete control, thanks to Magnet therapy and the medicine.*

Eye diseases like cataract and glaucoma, if in early stages, can be arrested or even reversed with Magnet therapy.

**Author's experience :** *One morning, Mr. Dattatrey Pathak from Dahanu came to me, with the complaint of hazy vision. He felt like seeing through a fog.*

*I examined his eyes. It was evident that he was suffering from incipient cataract. In spite of wearing correct glasses, he was able to read only five lines of the distant vision testing chart.*

*I advised him to use the magnetic device for eye-treatment for 15-30 minutes twice a day, bring about a few changes in his diet and visit me at monthly intervals.*

*The haze in front of his eyes gradually lessened. After three months, he was able to read seven lines of the vision testing chart. This clearly proved that the cataractous changes in the lens of his eyes had been reversed.*

In high blood pressure, the north pole of a medium power magnet, when kept below the right ear for 30 minutes, twice a day gives considerable relief.

In hyperthyroidism and hypothyroidism, the south and the north poles, respectively of strong magnets, have provided good results.

**Author's experience :** *32 year old Mrs. Shobha Parekh came to me one evening. From the various reports which she presented, it was evident that her thyroid gland was functioning subnormally. Her external experience (especially the swelling on her throat) and her complaints also supported the investigative findings.*

*Mrs. Parekh's mother had previously been under my treatment for her knee pain. She had suggested her daughter to consult me. Mrs. Parekh insisted Magnet therapy for her disorder.*

*I advised her to drink magnetised water and apply the north pole of a strong magnet to the base of her throat for 30 minutes, twice a day. Besides, I gave her a list of natural foods which were rich in iodine and asked her to consume them freely.*

*With this treatment plan, her condition gradually improved. At the end of about two months and a half, she was feeling quite healthy. The swelling on her throat, too, had disappeared. To ascertain that her disease had been overcome, she got her blood examined again. There were no abnormalities in the reports.*

Magnet therapy is useful for burns, too. For the first two or three days, an application of the south pole brings about pain-relief. Thereafter, if there is no infection, the use of the north pole brings about speedy healing.

Magnets have also proved useful in disorders of the kidneys and the urinary bladder. In many Russian hospitals, magnetised water is given to persons with kidney ailments. Magnetised water also has the power to break down and dissolve stones in kidneys or the urinary bladder.

**Author's experience :** *67-year old Mr. Indravadan Jani from Goregaon,* **Mumbai** *had been troubled by a stone in the urinary bladder for about two months. He suffered from abdominal pain and experienced acute pain while passing urine. Doctors had advised surgery. But Mr. Jani was of an apprehensive nature and was not prepared to undergo an operation.*

*Mr. Jani had heard about Magnet therapy and had even read my book on the subject.*

*He took home, a pair of strong magnets, for preparing magnetised water. On the twelfth day after commencing Magnet therapy, Mr. Jani experienced excruciating pain while passing urine. He was moved to tears. This pain was the result of the passing out of some tiny grains through his urinary tract. The stone had thus been broken down and expelled.*

*Mr. Jani's problem came to an immediate end after this dramatic event.*

If magnetised water (approx. 30 ml) is given at 10 minutes intervals to a person suffering from anuria (lack of urine), the crisis is overcome in an hour or an hour and a half.

Magnetised water improves digestion, lessens gastric acidity and cures flatulence.

*It is the author's experience that most patients of hyper-acidity, burning sensation in the stomach and peptic ulcers experience quick relief with magnetised water.*

Dr. A. K. Bhattacharya has presented an interesting fact in his book 'Magnet and Magnetic Field'. He once visited the factory of a leading manufacturer of magnets. A senior officer of the factory proudly stated that all the workers of the factory had only sons. Dr. Bhattacharya has requested the concerned authorities to investigate into this matter because the discovery may prove to be a boon to couples who have only daughters and who crave for a son.

Magnets beneficially affect the whole body. They succeed to favourably stimulate the endocrine glands, the blood, the digestive system, the nervous system, the urinary system and almost all the organs of the body.

**Summary :**

1. Scientists conducted experiments to determine whether the health-giving effects of magnets were produced in human beings as well.
2. These experiments yielded encouraging results. When magnets are kept in contact with a part of the body, the whole body is favourably influenced.
3. Magnets have given good results in such diseases which are not amenable to prevalent modes of treatment.
4. Cancerous growths, too, can be arrested by using suitable magnets.

# 9. FORCES THAT DISTURB THE BIOMAGNETIC FORCES INSIDE THE BODY AND CAUSE DISEASE

A disturbance of the natural vibratory frequency of the cells of an organ or a part of the body gives rise to a disease.

The factors discussed below cause such changes in the natural vibratory frequency. One should acquire the knowledge about these factors and try to keep away from them. Without such care, Magnet therapy may not give the desired results.

**External factors :**

(1) A change in electromagnetic field of the earth due to electromagnetic storms on the sun.

(2) A change in electromagnetic field of the earth due to storms, cyclones, pollution, sudden changes in weather etc.

(3) Natural radiations from the soil.

(4) Artificial radiations due to colour television, X-rays, leakage from atomic plants and testing of nuclear weapons.

It has been already discussed that bodies in space affect the life on the earth. Suicides, crimes and attacks of madness show a marked increase during full-moon and no-moon days.

During storms or cyclones, changes in the electro-magnetism, amounting to 50-milli volts have been recorded. Such high changes have an undesirable effect on persons with low resistance power. Such persons fall victims to diseases.

Natural radioactive substances, too, affect the body. An undesirable result of the giant strides in industrial progress is that atmospheric pollution has reached an all-time high level. Besides, the advanced countries frequently test their newly developed nuclear weapons and bombs. These factors cause fluctuations in earth's magnetic field and cause ill-health. The ghastly consequences of the American atomic attack on Hiroshima and Nagasaki in Japan are well-known.

Radiations cannot be experienced by human beings. That is the reason why one should stay away from unnecessary X-rays and even colour television-viewing. In an experiment, two similar plants were kept in front of a colour television. One plant was protected from the television rays by interposing a lead screen between the plant and the television. Within a few days, the plant exposed to television shrivelled and died. The protected plant was not affected.

**Internal factors :**

**(1) Faulty diet :** Diet can make a man; diet can also mar a man. Faulty diet is one of the chief factors which disturb the electromagnetic forces within the body.

Today, we do not eat to live but we live to eat. We have drifted away from nature and her foods. The consumption of frozen and canned foods, spicy and fried eatables and sweets is on the rise. It is no wonder that ill-health, too, is on the rise. We not only eat junk food, we eat it in large quantities too. With such unnatural food, one cannot expect to maintain a balance between the various electromagnetic forces within the body.

**(2) Irregular life :** Today's hectic activities have made our life irregular. Consequently, the natural biological rhythm is jeopardised. This, in turn, leads to inefficient bowel movements and constipation. It is a common belief that constipation is the mother of many an illness.

**(3) Addictions :**

Bad habits, too, cause an imbalance of the electromagnetic forces inside the body. Tea, coffee, tobacco, alcohol and drugs weaken the natural resistance power of the body. This resistance power depends upon vitamins. Tobacco, alcohol and drugs exhaust the valuable vitamins stored in our body. It has been found through experiments that almost 25 mg of vitamin C stored in our body is lost by smoking just one cigarette.

**(4) Lack of exercise :** Modern industrialisation has undermined the importance of physical exercise. Modern man hates manual work. Labourers are looked down upon and frowned at. Persons doing white collar jobs enjoy a high place in the society. This lack of physical exercise throws the digestive, the respiratory and the circulatory systems into disarray and causes disease.

**(5) Mental tension :** Mental tension today has exceeded all limits. It is the result of fast and competitive life. Like addictions, mental tension, too, destroys the vitamins stored inside the body and weakens the natural resistance power. That most diseases are rooted in mental tension is now unanimously accepted.

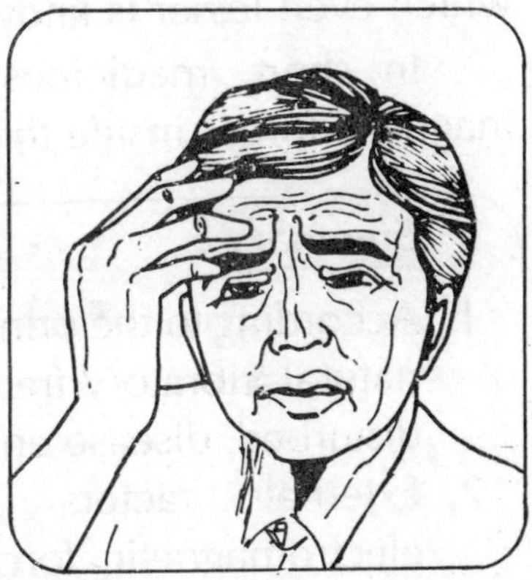

**(6) Indiscriminate use of medicines :** That medicines suppress the natural resistance power of the body is beyond dispute.

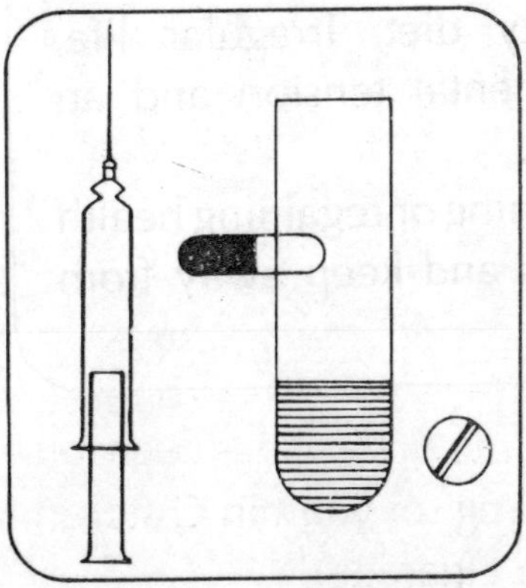

A medicine taken through the mouth is first digested. It is then absorbed through the intestines and mixes with the blood. Through blood circulation, it then reaches each and every cell of the body. Thus, the medicine not only reaches the diseased cells or organ but reaches all the body-cells. It is logical to think that a medicine which can destroy bacteria or other organisms can, to a greater or lesser extent, also harm other cells. Dr. Dale Friend, Professor of Medicine at the Harvard University and Chief of Clinical Pharmacology Department at the Britham Hospital in Boston, bluntly states that 'there is no such thing as a safe medicine'.

Our resistance to disease is based on white blood corpuscles. Medicines suppress the bone marrows which manufacture white blood corpuscles.

The renowned physician Dr. William Osler's statement is worth noting : 'A true doctor is the one who realises the futility of his drugs'. Very little is really known about drugs. Such ill-understood drugs are introduced into human bodies, about which even lesser is known.

In short, medicines, too, disturb the various electro-magnetic forces inside the body.

**Summary :**

1. According to the principle of Magnet therapy, when the natural vibratory frequency of a tissue or an organ is disturbed, disease ensues.
2. External factors which disturb the body's electromagnetic forces include sun-storms, eclipses, storms, cyclones, pollution and sudden changes in weather.
3. Internal factors which disturb the body's electro-magnetic forces include faulty diet, irregular life, addictions, a sedentary life, mental tension and an indiscriminate use of medicines.
4. Every person desirous of maintaining or regaining health should understand these factors and keep away from them.

# 10. HOW DO MAGNETS ACT ?

What changes occur inside the body when magnets are applied to a part of the body ? What is the mechanism by which the magnets produce their salubrious effects ? Scientists and physicians have put forward a number of theories.

It has been stated earlier that every cell and every organ of our body is a magnetic unit and has a specific vibratory frequency. When there is a perfect harmony between the vibratory frequencies of the various tissues and organs of the body, health is the natural consequence. If this harmony is lost because of changes in the natural vibratory frequency of an organ or a part of the body, disease ensues.

Most modes of treatment do not consider human body as a single unit. They treat each part of the body as a separate or independent entity. On the other hand, Magnet therapy considers the human body as one, indivisible unit. According to its principles, no organ of our body can be healthy or diseased, independent of the rest of the body. This is the reason why it aims at restoring health to not only that part of the body where the symptoms of disease externally appear, but to the entire body.

Magnet therapy strikes at the root of the disease. It strives to restore the natural vibratory frequency of the various organs and to re-establish a balance in their electromagnetic forces.

### How do magnets act ?

**(1) The direct effects of magnetism :** When magnets are kept in contact with a part of the body, the cells and organs of that part regain their natural vibratory frequency.

The electromagnetic waves emanating from the magnets are capable of very deep and extensive penetration and reach almost every cell of the concerned part of the body. The protoplasm of the cells gets polarised. Such polarisation imparts strength to the cells.

When magnets are placed near the body, the regeneration process in that part is stimulated. Old worn out cells are replaced by new, healthy ones. Therefore, a wound heals rapidly and a broken bone unites fast.

Magnets suppress the activities of harmful and disease-causing bacteria. They are rendered passive and weak, following which the natural resistance power of the body easily destroys them.

**(2) The indirect effects of magnetism :** A magnet affects the physical and chemical properties of liquids. Centres of crystallisation increase; the density, the viscosity, the surface tension are suitably altered.

Blood is also chiefly a fluid. It, too, is affected. Moreover, the red blood corpuscles, which contain iron, are attracted towards the magnet. Thus, the blood is also polarsied.

When electromagnetic waves enter the blood stream, eddy currents are produced. These eddy currents warm up the blood and increase the number of ions in the blood.

When such ion-rich, polarised and warm blood circulates, it produces health-giving effects on the whole body. It washes away the metabolic waste products that have accumulated in the muscles. Muscular tension, fatigue and pain are thus relieved. The deposits of cholesterol on the inner surface of the blood vessels are eroded and dissolved. Thus, blood supply to important organs improves. The warm blood stimulates the endocrine glands to function more efficiently.

In illnesses, especially infectious illnesses, the ESR and the number of white blood corpuscles increase. Following a few sessions of Magnet therapy, both these factors come down, signifying that the infection has come under control.

In short, magnetised blood rejuvenates and invigorates each and every cell of the body; the various systems of the body become more efficient; the body's natural resistance power improves.

All these are indirect effects of the magnets. Thus, the treatment, which appears local at the first sight, is in fact effective on the entire body.

**(3) Magnetised water :** Water influenced by magnets undergoes certain physical and chemical changes. Its physical properties like centres of crystallisation, pH (hydrogen ion concentration) and nitrogen dissolving capacity are suitably altered.

Such magnetised water, when consumed, improves health. It improves digestion and reduces acidity. It acts like a diuretic. It dissolves kidney-stones. Further details about magnetised water have been given in Chapter 11.

**Summary :**

1. When a magnet is kept in contact with (or near) a part of the body, the cells of that part undergo polarisation, the resistance power of that part is enhanced and illness is driven away.
2. Magnets suitably affect the blood. Such magnetised blood favourably affects the body. Since the blood continuously circulates, even local treatment with magnets produces effects on the whole body. Magnetised blood improves the various processes occurring in the body and the functioning of the endocrine glands. Consequently, health is regained.
3. Magnetised water, when consumed, has good effects on the digestive, the circulatory and the urinary systems.

# 11. MAGNETISED WATER

Substances can be classified into ferromagnetic, paramagnetic and diamagnetic.

Ferromagnetic substances are strongly attracted towards a magnet. Iron, nickel and cobalt are examples of ferromagnetic substances.

Paramagnetic substances are only mildly attracted towards a magnet. Water and other fluids are paramagnetic.

Diamagnetic substances move away from a magnet. Gold, silver, mercury, zinc etc. are examples of diamagnetic substances.

**Effects of magnetic field on water :** It has been seen during experiments that the magnetic field increases the centres of crystallisation in fluids. When exposed to á strong magnetic field, physical properties of water like density, viscosity, surface tension, electrical conductivity etc. and chemical properties like pH, nitrogen ion concentration undergo changes. Such water is termed 'magnetised water'.

A number of experiments have been conducted in many countries, especially Russia, to determine the effects of magnetised water on living as well as non-living things.

The 'water carrying capacity' of pipe-lines is gradually decreased by deposition of certain hard substances on the inner surface of pipes. This deposition reduces the efficiency of machines. A 1.5 mm thick layer of deposits on the inner surface of pipes reduces the efficiency of the combustion engine of a motor-car, by five horse power. This leads to an elevation of fuel costs and a reduction of the engine's life.

When magnetised water is passed through such 'blocked' pipes, the deposits are softened and gradually washed away. Thus,the pipes can be cleaned without hampering or stopping the work.

Motor-engineers have found 'magnetised water' useful. Such water, when introduced in the radiator, washes away existent deposits and prevents the formation of fresh deposits.

Magnetised water is also useful for construction work. When magnetised water is used, the strength of the cement concrete has been found to increase by 20-35 per cent. This cuts down the future maintenance costs.

Plants and trees irrigated with magnetised water grow 20 to 40 per cent faster and are stronger and bear heavy fruit.

Cows, when given magnetised water, yield more milk.

**The usefulness of magnetised water to man :** Magnetised water, when drunk, favourably affects the health.

Magnetised water is useful in most diseases especially those of the digestive, the excretory and the nervous systems.

Magnetised water improves digestion, reduces gastric acidity and cures flatulence. It is useful in constipation as well.

Magnetised water relieves women of their menstrual problems.

Magnetised water when consumed regularly prevents the deposition of cholesterol on the inner surface of blood vessels. It has also been seen to decrease cholesterol deposits when drunk for a long period. This brings about an improvement in blood-supply and nutrition to the various organs, including the heart.

Magnetised water is a diuretic and is useful in kidney troubles. A person suffering from anuria (no urination), when given magnetised water at intervals of ten minutes, experiences relief in an hour or two. Magnetised water can dissolve stones in the urinary system.

This water strengthens and invigorates the natural resistance power of the body. Hence it is useful for the treatment of viral diseases, common cold, influenza, cough, asthma and most other diseases.

There is a place called Evian in France, where people from all over Europe flock. Springs in Evian are believed to relieve joint troubles, obesity and urinary disorders. This 'Evian water' is even bottled and sold all over France. It finds a place in all homes and hotels of France. This 'Evian water' is nothing but naturally magnetised water. In our country, too, there are such springs where persons in ill-health flock to regain health.

Like water, milk too can be magnetised and its nutritional value enhanced.

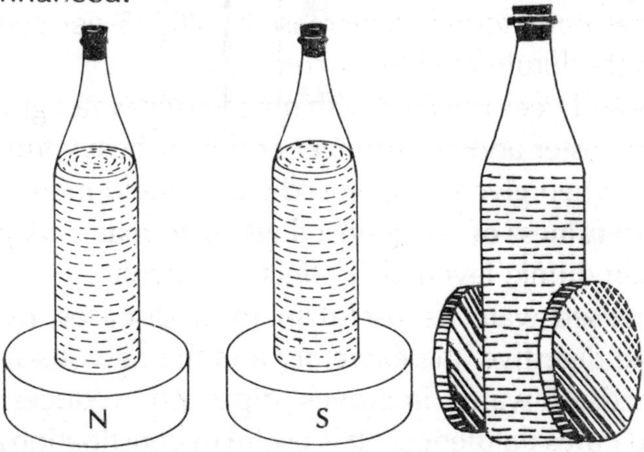


**How to magnetise water? :** Strong magnets are necessary to magnetise water. Such strong magnets should be kept in contact with a glass or plastic bottle (or a glass) containing water. This contact should be maintained for about 24 hours. However, if need be, water influenced for 12-14 hours can also be used.

Usually, water influenced by both the poles (north as well as south) simultaneously should be consumed. For preparing such water, two magnets should be placed on either side of a bottle containing water such that the north pole of one magnet faces the south pole of the other magnet.

Water, magnetised by only one pole, may have to be used in specific problems. For example, in hyperacidity or gastric ulcer, water magnetised by south pole alone should be used. On the other hand, for sluggish digestion, water magnetised with north pole alone can be used.

It should be noted that for magnetising water, the magnets are to be kept in contact with the water-bottle from outside; they are not to be immersed into the water.

Magnetised water should not be heated or kept in a refrigerator.

Once influenced by magnets, the water remains magnetised for about three to four days.

**The dosage of magnetised water :** Magnetised water should be taken three to five times a day, in doses of about 100 ml (half a glass). Small children may be given a lesser quantity of water each time.

Magnetised water can also be used to wash eyes, to cleanse wounds and burns and to flush the intestines (through an enema).

**Summary :**

1. Water, when kept in contact with magnets for at least 12 hours, gets magnetised.
2. Magnetised water has healing properties.
3. Magnetised water can be used by the healthy and the sick alike. Healthy persons can drink this water to enhance their natural resistance power and thereby maintain health. They can also keep their digestive system efficient with the help of this water.

   Magnetised water cleans up the deposits of cholesterol from the inner surface of blood vessels, decreases gastric acidity, soothes gastric ulcers, dissolves stones in the urinary system, cures menstrual disorders in women and stimulates development in children.
4. During epidemics, magnetised water prevents a person from contracting the infection.
5. Usually, water magnetised with both the poles simultaneously should be drunk. However, if a need is felt, water magnetised with either the north or the south pole alone, can be consumed.
6. Besides drinking, magnetised water can be favourably used in a number of other ways. It can be given to plants and to domestic animals to maintain their health. It can be used to wash eyes and wounds. It can be used to soothe pain in burns and to prevent the formation of blisters.

## 12. MAGNETISED OIL

Medicinal oils and hair-oils, too, can be magnetised and rendered more useful.

**Oil influenced with both the poles :** Take a glass bottle, preferably rectangular and fill it up with the required oil. Keep strong magnets in contact with this bottle such that north pole of one magnet faces the south pole of the other magnet. Retain such contact for about 15 days. By this period, the oil gets magnetised.

Such oil, magnetised by both the poles simultaneously, is recommended for general use, i.e., for applying to hair, for massaging babies and for instilling in the nose and ears.

**Oil influenced with the north pole alone :** In this method, only the north pole of a strong magnet should be kept in contact with the bottle containing oil. The magnet should preferably be positioned such that it faces the north direction.

This oil is recommended as a massage-medium in general weakness, paralysis and baldness.

**Oil influenced with south pole alone :** To prepare such an oil, only the south pole of a strong magnet should be kept in contact with the oil-bottle. The magnet should be positioned to face the south direction.

This oil is recommended as a massage-medium in joint disorders, pain, skin problems and insomnia (scalp massage).

Rose water, tonics, eye-drops and other liquids also can be magnetised and rendered more useful and effective.

Rose-water magnetised with the south pole can be used as eye-drops.

Milk, magnetised for a few minutes with the north pole, if drunk at night, enhances sexual ability.

**Summary :**

1. Like water, oil, too, can be magnetised.
2. Generally, the oil magnetised with both the poles together should be used.
3. North-magnetised oil is more effective in paralysis, baldness or general weakness.
4. South-magnetised oil is more effective in pain, ear ailments, skin troubles and arthritis.
5. If north-magnetised milk is consumed at night, it increases vitality and sexual powers.

# 13. THE PRINCIPLES OF APPLYING MAGNETS FOR TREATMENT

Magnets were used for treatment purposes in ancient times, too. But their use was sporadic. Methodical and scientific use of magnets for the treatment of various diseases was commenced only some 40-50 years back.

Thus, the science of Magnet therapy is still in its infancy. That is the reason why there is no unanimity in the method of application of magnets for treatment. Depending upon their experiments and experiences, various physicians use magnets in different ways. It is heartening to note that all of them have encountered success in spite of the differences in the methods.

It is quite evident that, whatever be the method of application, magnets affect the whole body, besides the part adjacent to which they are placed. Moreover, no method has been found to cause any serious harm, i.e., to say Magnet therapy produces no undesirable side-effects.

There are two important methods of applying magnets : (1) The unipolar method, where only one pole (either the south or the north) is used at a time and (2) The bipolar method, where both the poles are used simultaneously. Before elaborating on these two modes of treatment, it would be worthwhile to consider the properties of the two poles.

**Properties of the south pole :** (1) The south pole is inhibitory and suppressive. (2) It imparts coolness and peace. (3) If kept in water for some time, it makes the water slightly alkaline. In short, it decreases the acidity of fluids. (4) It produces contraction and shrinkage of body-tissues. (5) It slows down the circulation in small blood-vessels and capillaries. (6) It inhibits the activity of bacteria, controls infection and decreases inflammation (swelling). (7) It arrests growth of boils, carbuncles and tumours. (8) It checks the ripening of fruits and vegetables and acts to retain their freshness. (9) It decreases pain. (10) It brings down the body-temperature.

Thus, the south pole is useful in infectious and inflammatory conditions. It is commonly used in skin conditions, arthritis, infectious diseases, tumours, anxiety, convulsions, eye ailments, pain, neuralgia, insomnia and a number of other disorders.

**Properties of the north pole :** (1) The north pole possesses stimulatory or augmentative properties. (2) It imparts warmth and energy. (3) If placed in water for some time, it renders the water slightly acidic. In short, it increases the acidity of fluids. (4) It produces expansion of body-tissues. (5) It speeds up the circulation in small blood vessels and capillaries. (6) It encourages the activity and growth of bacteria, worsens infections and increases swelling. (7) It stimulates the growth of boils and tumours. (8) It hastens the ripening of fruits and vegetables. (9) It has little effect on pain and sometimes makes it more acute. (10) It increases the body-temperature.

The energy, strength and warmth-giving properties of the north pole can be utilised to treat paralysis, hernia, leucoderma, baldness, muscle weakness, general weakness, unconsciousness and a number of other disorders.

Since the north and the south poles have opposing properties, correctly recognising the poles of an unknown magnet is of paramount importance.

Suspend the magnet freely with a light thread. Allow it to stabilise. That surface or end of the magnet which points towards the north direction is the 'north-seeking' or simply the 'North' pole. That surface or end of the magnet which points towards the south direction is the 'south-seeking' or simply the 'South' pole. This method of naming or marking the magnetic poles finds universal acceptance from physicists. Label the magnet with the letters 'N' and 'S'. With the help of this magnet, the poles of any other unknown magnet can be correctly determined from the property of magnets which can be stated as 'like poles repel and unlike poles attract'.

The use of only one pole of the magnet for the treatment of disease is obviously more logical. But before commencing such 'unipolar' treatment it is necessary to correctly diagnose the disease. This is very important because an incorrect diagnosis may lead to an use of the incorrect pole of the magnet, resulting into a failure to cure the disease or ameliorate the symptoms.

Some physicians have resorted to using both the poles simultaneously for treating any disease. This method, too, may yield results. But it remains a fact that the results are very slow and sometimes unsatisfactory.

The pioneer in the field of biomagnetics Dr. Albert Roy Davis of America and Dr. A. K. Bhattacharya are staunch supporters of the unipolar method of treatment. They have proved time and again that this unipolar method of treatment succeeds even when the bipolar method has failed.

However, bipolar method should be employed whenever there are clear indications for doing so. For example, if the part of the body to be treated is painful as well as weak or stiff, both the poles can be used simultaneously. Albeit, the part should have no active infection. In such treatment, better results are obtained if the north pole is positioned to face the north and the south pole is positioned to face the south direction.

The north and the south poles can also be used one after the other, during a single treatment session. In injury, spinal pain, low backache etc., treatment with the south pole for the first 10-20 minutes and with the north pole for the next 10-20 minutes may be desirable. This method resembles the alternate hot and cold baths, also termed contrast baths, advocated by Nature cure practitioners.

One point needs further elucidation here. Some physicians treat each and every disease by keeping the magnets in contact with the patient's palms and the soles.

It is necessary to consider the changes that occur in the body, when the magnets are applied in this fashion.

(1) When the north pole is kept in contact with the right palm (or sole) and the south pole is kept in contact with the left

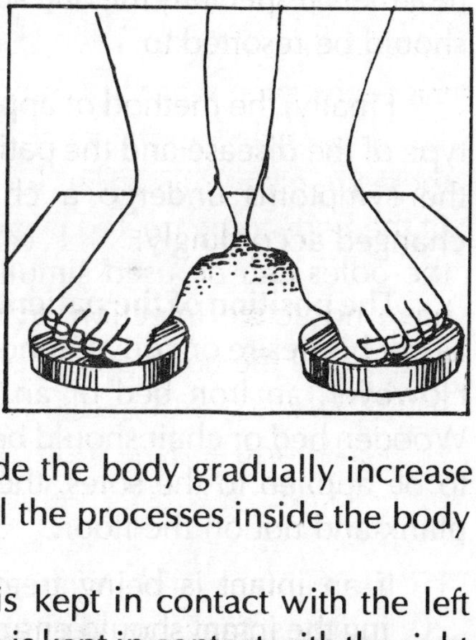

palm (or sole), cool forces inside the body gradually increase and dominate. Consequently, all the processes inside the body slow down.

(2) When the north pole is kept in contact with the left palm (or sole) and the south pole is kept in contact with the right palm (or sole), hot forces inside the body gradually increase and predominate. Consequently, all the processes inside the body are paced up.

In conditions like fever, excessive perspiration, allergy, high blood pressure, rheumatoid arthritis and hyperthyroidism, the first type of treatment (i.e., the one which stimulates the cool forces) may prove useful.

In conditions like frost-bite, paralysis, varicose veins, obesity, diabetes and hypothyroidism, the second type of treatment (i.e., the one which stimulates the hot forces of the body) may prove useful.

But resorting to such treatment (i.e., applying magnets to the palms and the soles) in each and every disease is illogical. Propounding the theory or the formula that any disease of the upper part of the body can be treated through the palms and any disease of the lower part of the body can be treated through the soles is ill-founded and misleading.

It is not the authors' aim to ridicule this method of treatment. But when expected results are not obtained by the above-mentioned method of treatment, other logical methods of treatment (especially the one advocating the use of a single pole) should be resorted to.

Finally, the method of applying magnets depends upon the type of the disease and the patient's symptoms. If the disease or the symptoms undergo a change, the treatment should be changed accordingly.

**The position of the patient :** The patient can sit or lie down as per his desire or convenience and the needs of the treatment. However, an iron bed or an iron chair should not be used. Wooden bed or chair should be used instead. If the magnets are to be applied to the soles, they should be kept on a wooden plank and not on the floor.

If an infant is being treated, the person (or the mother) ·ing the infant should ensure a 'no-contact' with the floor.

During the treatment, the magnets should preferably be positioned such that the north pole faces the north direction and the south pole faces the south direction. In such a position, the field of the magnets is parallel to that of the earth and better results accrue.

During treatment, it is not necessary to remove the clothes from the concerned part because the magnetic field can easily pass through the clothes. In fact, the waves can even penetrate glass, rubber or wood.

**The choice of magnets :** The shape, the size and the power of the magnet selected for treatment depend upon the need and convenience.

(1) Delicate sensitive or like the eyes, small organs the brain and the heart should not be treated with strong magnets. A small round or rectangular magnet with a central hole would be ideal for treating such organs.

(2) Superficial diseases (e.g., a skin-ailment) do not call for very strong magnets. However, if the disease is deep-seated, strong magnets may have to be used.

(3) Strong magnets may be required for old and chronic diseases. Acute diseases, however, can be treated with weak or medium-power magnets.

**The duration of treatment :** Generally, in the initial stages, a 15 minute treatment session, once a day is adequate. For infants, 5-10 minutes may prove enough.

For chronic diseases, joint-disorders, paralysis and other such serious diseases, the duration of a treatment session may have to be gradually increased to 30-45 minutes. Later on, in such conditions, the treatment can even be had two or three times a day. In short, the duration of a single treatment depends upon the kind of disease and the condition of the patient.

It is difficult to judge the total period of treatment, i.e., for how long the treatment will have to be continued. It depends upon the type of disease, the length of the disease, the status of patient's recuperative powers, whether the patient stays away from disease-causing factors or not, etc. Developing correct dietary habits and maintaining cheerfulness also determine, to some extent, the speed of recovery. Mental tension can disturb the electromagnetic forces inside the body. Thus, during the course of treatment, if a new cause for mental tension arises, the improvement may be slowed down.

It is desirable that the first treatment with magnets is undertaken under the supervision of a physician.

**Can the treatment be taken at any time? :** If strong magnets are to be used for treatment, it is desirable that the stomach be empty. In other words, the treatment should be taken early in the morning or mid-morning or early evening.

Knee-pain, neck-pain and backache get worse in the evening, following the day's work. In such cases, the treatment should be preferably had in the evening.

Morning time is preferable for the treatment of digestive troubles like constipation, loose motions and colitis.

According to the principles of Ayurveda, the ailments of 'cough' like cold, cough and bronchitis are more acute in the morning; the ailments of 'pitta' become more acute in the midday; the ailments of 'vata' become more acute in the evening. These facts, too, can be taken into account, while deciding upon the time of treatment.

In short, if pain or other symptoms trouble the patient more at a particular time of the day, the treatment can be undertaken at that time.

There are no serious side-effects of magnetic treatment. However, a very sensitive individual may feel a mild headache, nausea or giddiness during the first few days of treatment. If one desires to be relieved of these symptoms immediately, he can do so by placing his palms or soles on a zinc plate for a few minutes.

**Some practical hints for treatment :**

(1) It is desirable to desist from taking magnetic treatment for two hours following a heavy meal; otherwise nausea or vomiting may result.

(2) Eyes, brain and heart should be treated only with weak magnets and for a shorter period of time (i.e. not exceeding 15-20 minutes).

(3) Pregnant women should usually not be treated with magnets. If magnetic treatment is extremely necessary, only weak magnets should be used, away from the uterus.

<u>**Summary**</u> :

1. The properties of the south pole and the north pole are mutually opposite.
2. There are two prevalent methods of using magnets : (a) the unipolar method and (b) the bipolar method.
3. It is more logical to apply only one pole to the diseased organ. This method gives more rapid and satisfactory results. However, it is necessary to correctly diagnose the disease because only then can a correct selection of the pole of the magnet be done.
4. Simultaneous use of both the poles may also give results. But improvement, with such treatment, is slow and many a time incomplete. However, in select cases, such treatment can be resorted to.
5. During treatment, the patient should be made to sit or lie down on a wooden chair or a bed.
6. In magnetic treatment, the shape or size of the magnet is of little importance. It can be selected as per the need or convenience.
7. For acute diseases or sensitive organs, weak magnets should be used. For chronic or deep-seated diseases, strong magnets may have to be used.

# 14. THE ADVANTAGES OF MAGNET THERAPY

The use of antibiotics and other medicines is fraught with danger. The side-effects of these medicines are more painful and troublesome than the disease itself. Many a time the body opposes these medicines. This is termed as hyper-sensitivity or allergy. The allergic response is sometimes so strong as to prove fatal. On the other hand, Magnet therapy is an external mode of treatment which does not play with the various chemicals and enzymes present inside the body. Moreover, it follows the laws of nature. Consequently, it is absolutely safe and harmless. Side-effects are unknown with Magnet therapy.

Allopathy gives good results in acute diseases. Ayurveda and Homoeopathy give good results in chronic and old illnesses. But Magnet therapy is effective in acute and chronic diseases alike. Many a time, cases or diseases not cured by other forms of treatment have been seen to respond to Magnet therapy. Cancer, joint disorders, insomnia, eczema, high blood pressure and a number of other illnesses, considered difficult to treat with modern medicines, are amenable to Magnet therapy. Results in some cases can be termed nothing but miracles.

Magnet therapy is not a slow or a long-term treatment. Sometimes the results obtained are immediate and dramatic. e.g., toothache can usually be relieved in just 10-15 minutes with the south pole of a strong magnet. Even when the improvement seems slow, as happens in chronic and long-standing diseases, it is permanent.

Magnet therapy is quite simple. It can be employed for patients of any sex or age.

No preparation is essential before commencing Magnet therapy.

The same magnet (or magnets) can be used by all the family members. Even then, the magnets need little care in the form of cleaning or sterilisation. However, when treating a skin-disease, due care should be taken. If a thin cloth is interposed between the skin and the magnet, the latter need not be cleaned.

Magnetic treatment can be undertaken at one's own home, saving the time spent in travelling to a doctor or a hospital. Besides, the treatment can be had at one's own convenient time.

Once purchased, the magnets can be used for years together because they retain their power for a long time. This means that Magnet therapy brings an end to recurring expenditure towards medicines and doctors.

Magnetic treatment is not addictive. No harm arises even if Magnet therapy is given up abruptly.

The most important point in favour of Magnet therapy is that with its assistance, diseases can be easily prevented and health maintained. During epidemics, magnets may save the person (or his family) from the infectious disease. Magnetised water, too, helps to achieve this goal.

Magnets may also be used to disperse fatigue and irritation, which result from the day-long work.

Finally, magnets also help a person to keep away senility and retain his youth for ever. This results from the fact that magnets impart energy, slow down the degenerative processes of the body and prevent (or reverse) the deposition of cholesterol in blood vessels. Thus the blood vessels remain flexible and broad, supply the various organs of the body with adequate nourishment and combat unwanted elements and toxins. That the life of animals can be prolonged and gray hair can be transformed to black again is a testimony to the fact that magnets can prevent ageing. This property of the magnets has been discussed in details in Chapter 15.

**Summary :**

1. Magnet therapy enjoys some advantages over other modes of treatment.
2. Magnet therapy is equally effective in acute as well as chronic illnesses.
3. The young and the old, a man or a woman, every person can avail of this simple, harmless and effective mode of treatment.
4. Magnets serve their owners for years, like faithful servants.
5. Magnets can prolong life and prevent senility.

## 15. CAN MAGNETS PREVENT OLD AGE ?

Everybody wants to stay young. Nobody likes old age and the things associated with it. Therefore, the search for elixir or 'amrit' which will keep man young for ever and will defer death, goes on and on. Ayurveda, too, recommends preparations which do 'Kayakalpa' i.e., rejuvenate the body.

It has been stated earlier that a house-fly's life-span could be doubled with magnets and a rat's life-span could be increased by about 45 per cent.

Dr. Maclean, a gynaecologist from America, has performed a number of clinical experiments on various human diseases, especially cancer, with magnets. He found to his amazement that besides curing the disease, the magnets bestowed other benefits, too. In some cases, grey hair of his old patients was found to revert to the original black or brown colour. This was nothing but restoration of youth by magnets.

Ageing brings about certain undesirable changes in the body. Menopause is one such change. It causes a great deal of embarrassment and shock to the affected woman. Studies have indicated that this ageing is brought about by a hormone secreted by the pituitary gland.

The resistance power of the body depends, to some extent, upon some cells including the T-lymphocytes manufactured by the thymus gland. These cells destroy the external germs which enter the body. After adolescence, the thymus gland gradually becomes inactive. Therefore, aged persons contract infections more easily than young persons. Scientists believe that the thymus gland is rendered inactive by the pituitary gland. The pituitary gland is considered responsible for suppressing the secretions of the thyroid gland, too. This has been proved by the experimental removal of the pituitary gland in animals. When the pituitary gland of old rats is removed, they have been seen to regain youth to a certain extent.

But the human pituitary gland cannot be removed, because this gland serves other useful purposes as well. However, the activity of the pituitary gland can be adequately controlled by magnets.

It is well-known that constant mental tension untowardly affects the body. The ageing hormone is secreted in greater quantities in a tense person. An overnight graying of hair following a tremendous shock is a known occurrence. On the other hand, people who take life lightly and who do not allow emotions to rule their heads succeed in keeping senility at bay.

The pituitary gland can be controlled and mental peace can be maintained (or attained) with the south pole of a magnet. Scientists have claimed that if the south pole of a weak magnet is applied to the forehead for about 15-30 minutes daily, ageing can be postponed and life can be prolonged. During the night, if a flat magnet is kept underneath the pillow, with its south pole facing upwards, it will keep the person's mind in peace, resulting into a deep and sound sleep. It will also effectively keep away other electromagnetic disturbances, to which we are liable.

Consumption of magnetised water, too, may contribute to the maintenance of youth.

Besides, a regular and addiction-free life, a frugal and light diet, yogasanas (especially Shavasana) and Acupressure treatment may also contribute to enable a person to lead a long yet youthful life.

<u>**Summary :**</u>

1. Magnets may help to slow down the ageing process, to which every person is liable.
2. Applying the south pole of a magnet to the forehead every day results into the dispersion of mental tension and a control on the activity of the pituitary gland. Consequently, ageing can be checked.
3. Magnetised water, too, can assist in slowing down the ageing process and maintaining youth.

# 16. PRACTICAL HINTS ABOUT THE USE AND PRESERVATION OF MAGNETS

**Preservation of magnets :**

(1) Magnets should not be allowed to clash with each other or to fall; otherwise steel magnets may loose their power and ceramic magnets may break.

(2) Magnets should preferably be kept in a wooden case or a wooden cupboard, when not in use.

(3) Steel magnets should not be allowed to get wet to prevent them from rusting. Similarly, the part of the body to which the magnet is to be applied should be completely wiped free of sweat.

**Hints for treatment :**

(1) Such time should be selected for treatment, when the stomach is not full.

(2) Sensitive or small organs like the brain, the heart and the eyes should not be treated with strong magnets.

(3) Pregnant women should be treated with weak magnets, if at all. The magnets should be placed away from the uterus.

(4) During treatment with magnets such metallic things (e.g., a wrist-watch) should not be worn on the body, which would absorb the magnetic waves.

(5) While treating skin-ailments, a cloth should be interposed between the skin and the magnet.

(6) A loose contact of the magnet with the body is sufficient; firm contact or pressure is not necessary. Albeit, the magnet should remain stationary.

(7) Big and strong magnets can be used once or twice daily for treatment. Small and weak magnets can even be continuously stuck to the body with the help of sticking plaster.

(8) Opposite poles of strong magnets should not be brought too close to each other. Otherwise the strong attraction might result into a clash, harming the magnets or crushing the

fingers that happen to come in between. Moreover, it may be difficult to separate the magnets later on.

(9) Homoeopathic drugs should not be kept in the vicinity of magnets because the latter cause changes in the potency of drugs.

(10) During a treatment session, it is desirable that the patient be seated or made to lie down parallel to the earth's magnetic field, i.e., in the north-south direction.

(11) During treatment, the patient should sit or lie down on a wooden chair or a bed.

# SECTION II : MAGNET THERAPY IN PRACTICE

## 17. PAIN

**(1) Headache :**

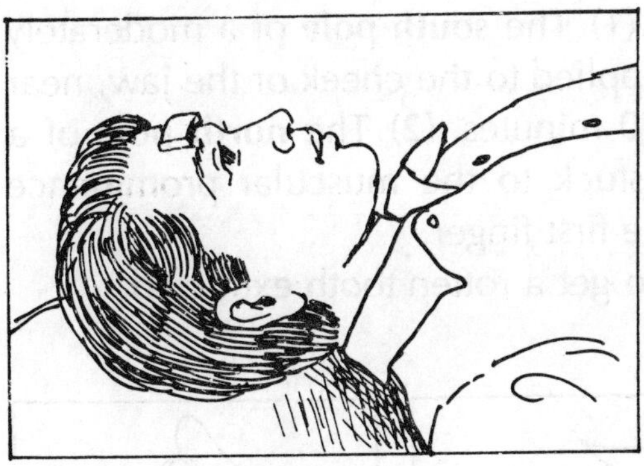

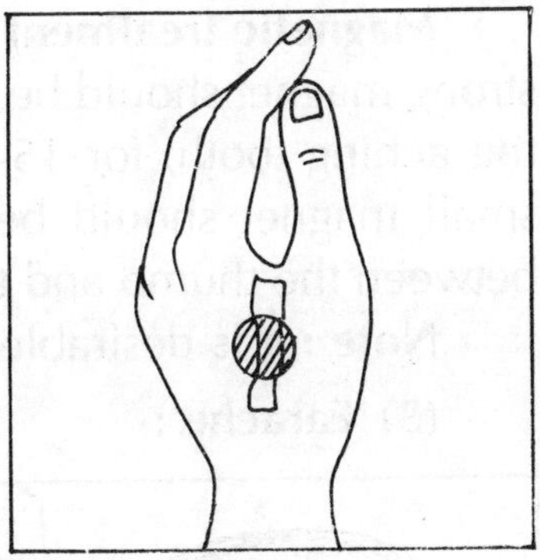

**Magnetic treatment** : (1) The **south pole** of a weak magnet should be applied to the forehead for 15-30 minutes, as and when required. Usually, one treatment proves sufficient. If not, it may be repeated after an hour or two. (2) For persistent or recurring headache repeat the treatment 2-3 times a day and stick (with a sticking tape) the **north pole** of a very small magnet to the muscular prominence between the thumb and the first finger. (3) Magnetised water should be drunk 4-5 times a day.

**Note** : Steps should also be taken to relieve mental tension, constipation or colds.

**(2) Toothache :**

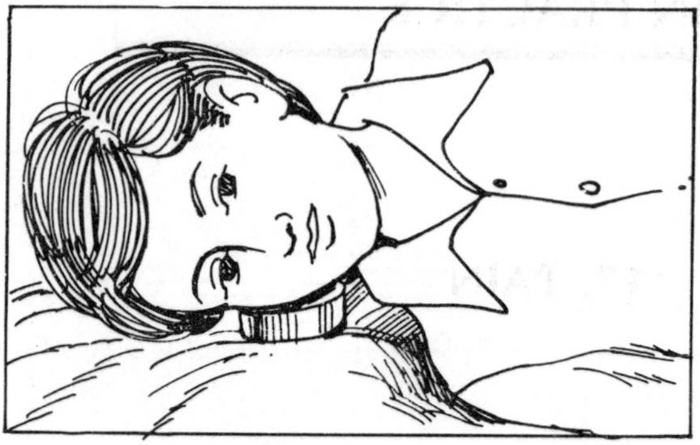

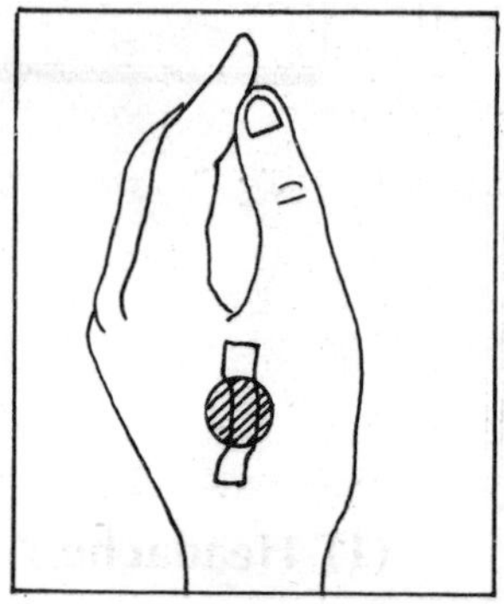

**Magnetic treatment :** (1) The **south pole** of a moderately strong magnet should be applied to the cheek or the jaw, near the aching tooth, for 15-30 minutes. (2) The **north pole** of a small magnet should be stuck to the muscular prominence between the thumb and the first finger.

**Note :** It is desirable to get a rotten tooth extracted.

**(3) Earache :**

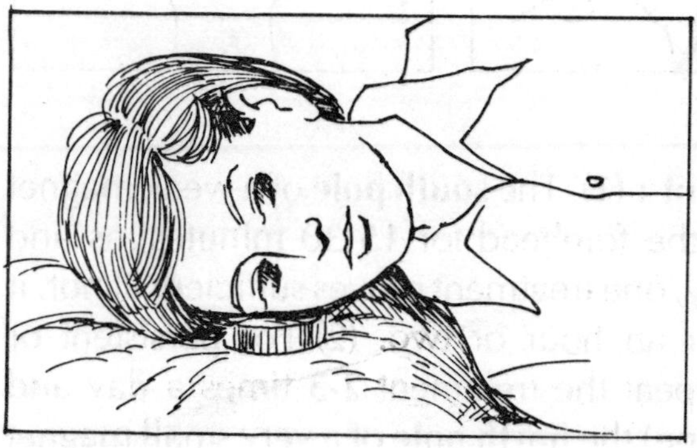

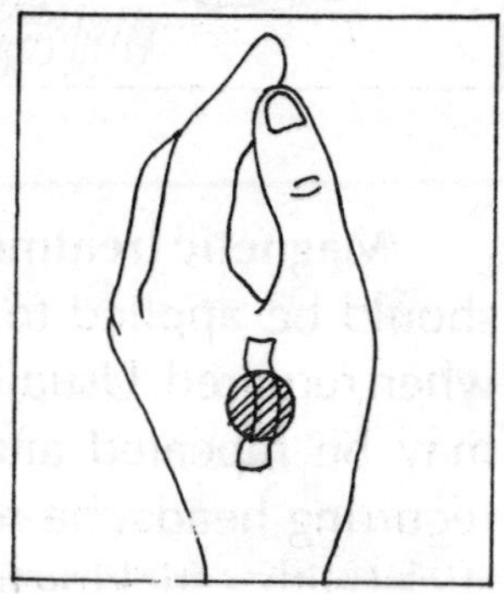

**Magnetic treatment :** (1) The **south pole** of a moderately strong magnet should be applied to the ear for 15-30 minutes, 2-3 times a day. (2) The **north pole** of a small magnet should be stuck to the muscular prominence between the thumb and the first finger. (3) Oil magnetised with the **south pole** should be dropped into the affected ear.

**Note :** If the pain is severe or if pus oozes out of the ear, a specialist should be consulted without delay.

**(4) Neck pain :**

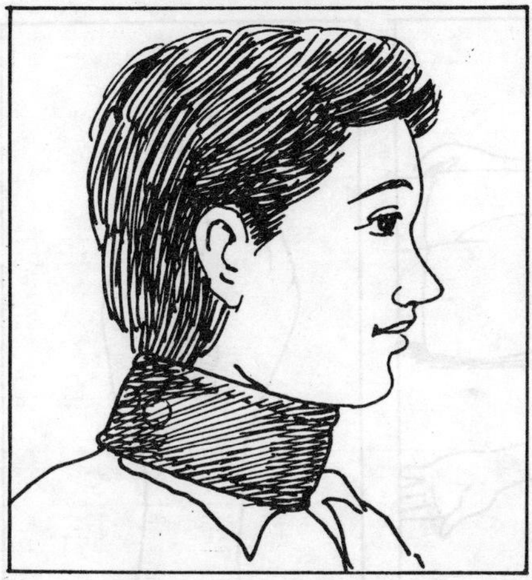

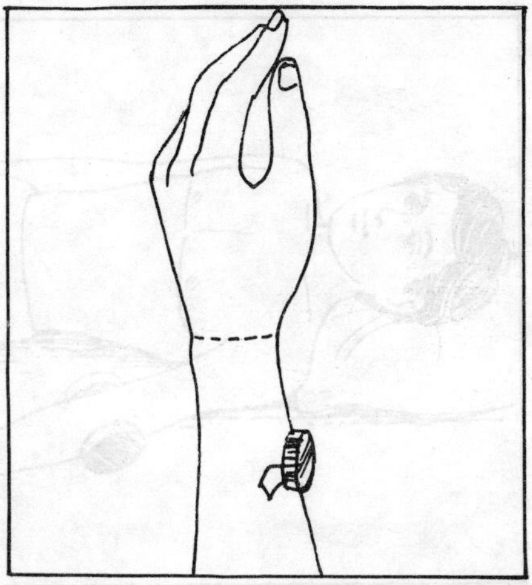

**Magnetic treatment :** (1) The **south pole** of a moderately strong magnet (or the magnetic neck belt) should be applied to the paining part of the neck for 15-30 minutes, 2-3 times a day. (2) The **north pole** of a small magnet should be stuck to the outer edge of the wrist joint, in line with the thumb.

**(5) Shoulder pain :**

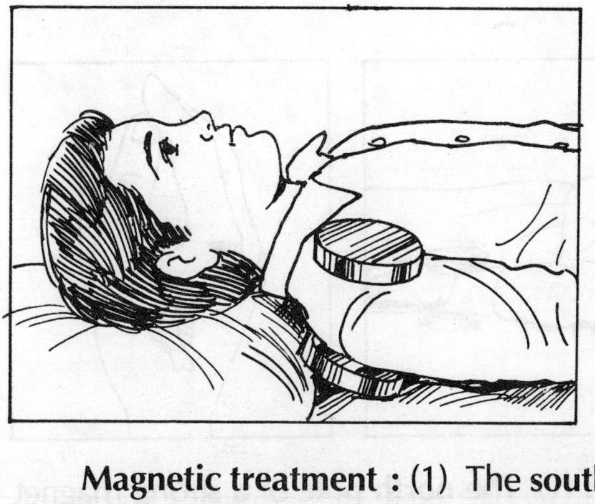

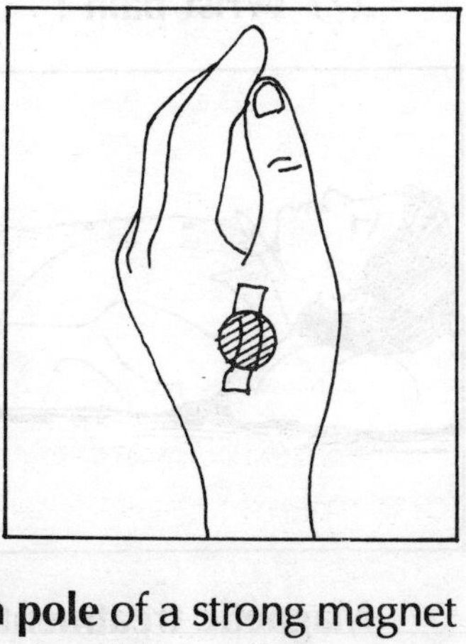

**Magnetic treatment :** (1) The **south pole** of a strong magnet should be applied to the front side of the shoulder and the **north pole** to the back side, for 15-30 minutes, 2-3 times a day. (2) The **north pole** of a small magnet should be stuck to the muscular prominence between the thumb and the first finger.

**(6) Elbow pain :**

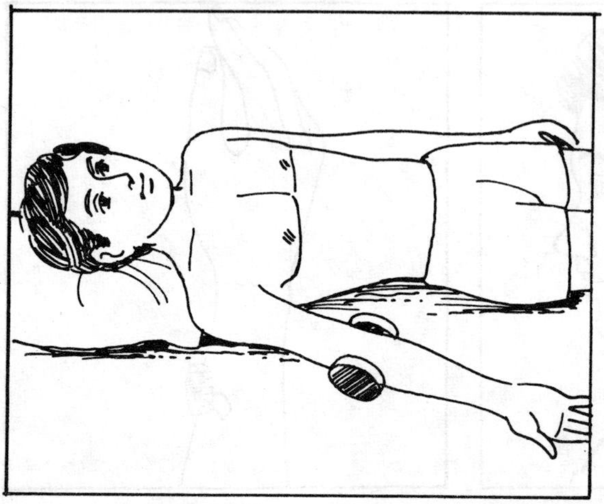

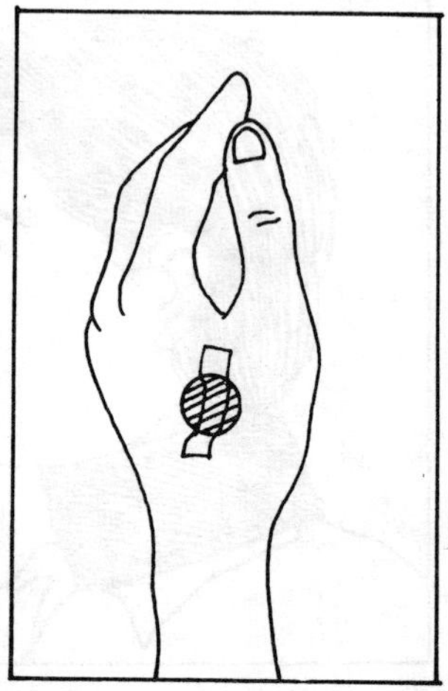

**Magnetic treatment :** (1) The **south pole** of a strong magnet should be applied to one side of the elbow and the **north pole** to the other, for 15-30 minutes, 2-3 times a day. (2) The **north pole** of a small magnet should be stuck to the muscular prominence between the thumb and the first finger.

**(7) Wrist pain :**

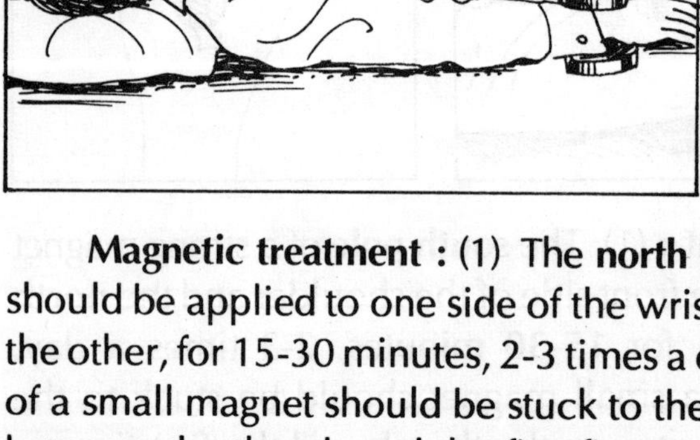

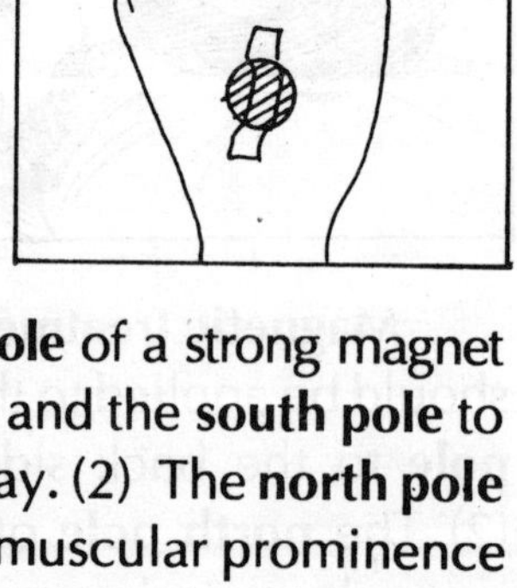

**Magnetic treatment :** (1) The **north pole** of a strong magnet should be applied to one side of the wrist and the **south pole** to the other, for 15-30 minutes, 2-3 times a day. (2) The **north pole** of a small magnet should be stuck to the muscular prominence between the thumb and the first finger.

## (8) Backache :

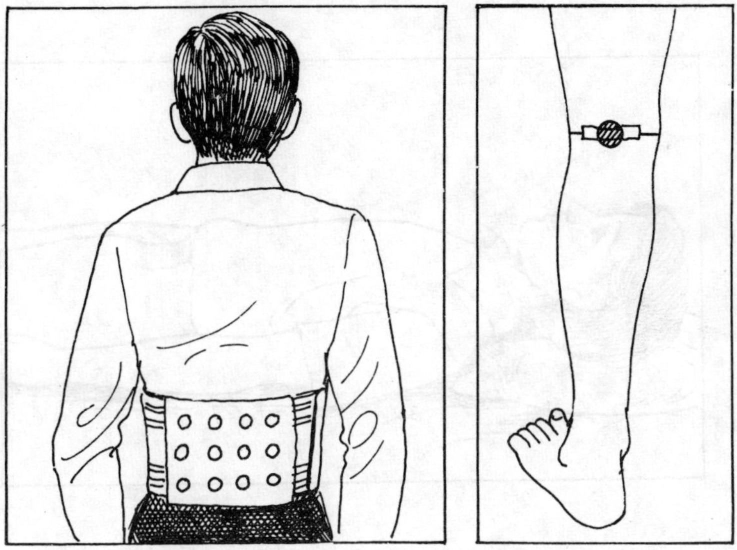

**Magnetic treatment :** (1) The paining area should be treated with the south pole (or both poles) of strong magnet, for 15-30 minutes, 2-3 times a day. (2) The **north pole** of a small magnet should be stuck to the mid-point of the dark crease found behind the knee.

**Note :** (1) A magnetic waist belt is more convenient and effective than loose magnets. (2) Refrain from stooping forward during day-to-day activities; do not lift heavy objects; perform exercises or asanas (e.g. Bhujangasana, Shalabhasana) which bend the spine backward. (3) Sleep on a very firm mattress; use only a single thin pillow.

**(9) Hip joint pain :**

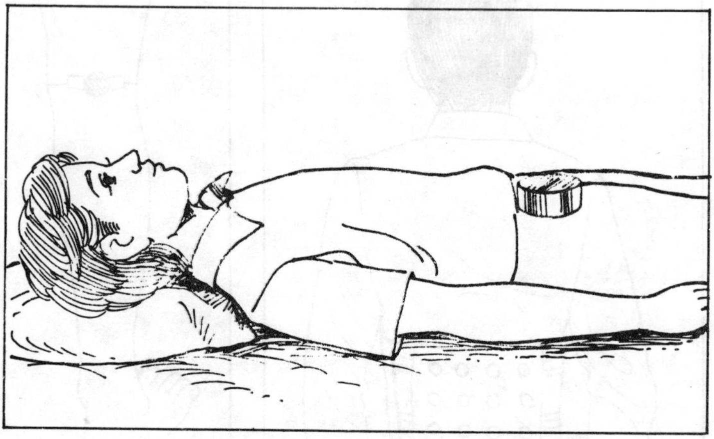

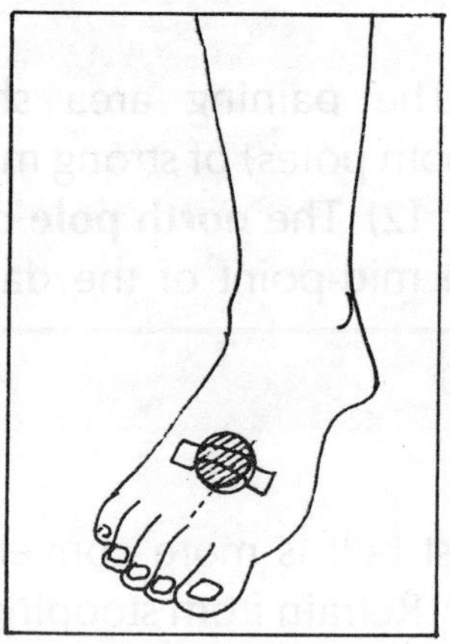

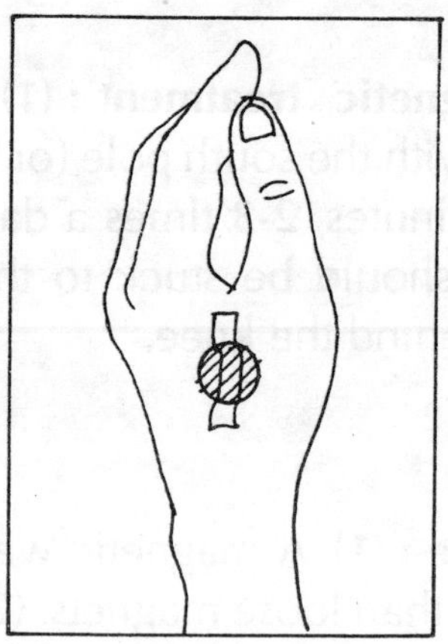

**Magnetic treatment :** (1) The **south pole** of a strong magnet should be applied to the front side of the paining hip, for 15-30 minutes, 2-3 times a day. (2) The **north pole** of a small magnet should be stuck to the muscular prominence, between the thumb and the first finger. (3) The **north pole** of another small magnet should be stuck to the web between the second toe (the one adjacent to the big toe) and the third toe.

**(10) Knee pain :**

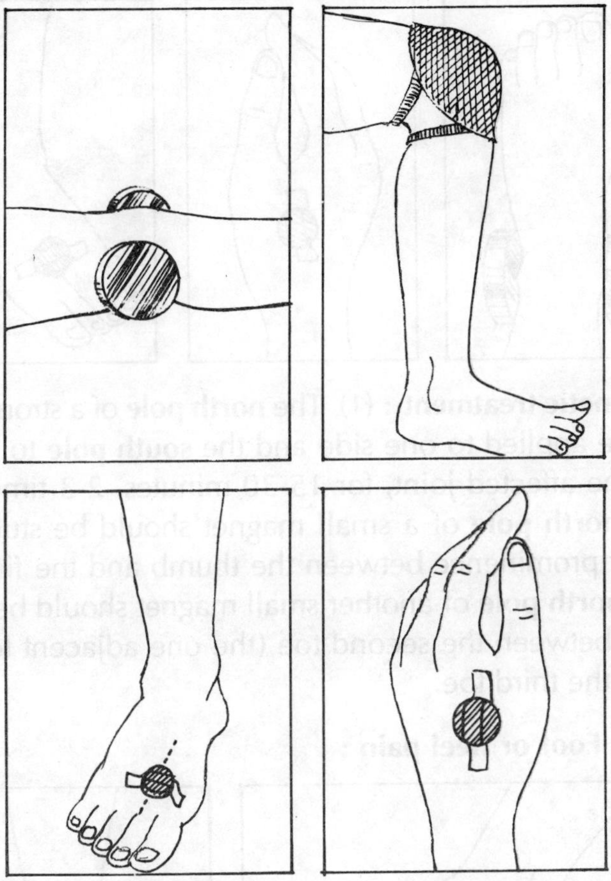

**Magnetic treatment :** (1) The **south pole** (or both poles) of strong magnets should be applied to the knee for 15-30 minutes, 2-3 times a day. (2) The **north pole** of a small magnet should be stuck to the muscular prominence between the thumb and the first finger. (3) The **north pole** of another small magnet should be stuck to the web between the second toe (the one adjacent to the big toe) and the third toe.

**Note :** (1) Magnetic knee belt proves more convenient and effective than loose magnets. (2) Body-weight, if excessive, should be reduced. (3) If pain is very acute, hot fomentation should be resorted to; but any massage should be strictly avoided.

**(11) Ankle pain :**

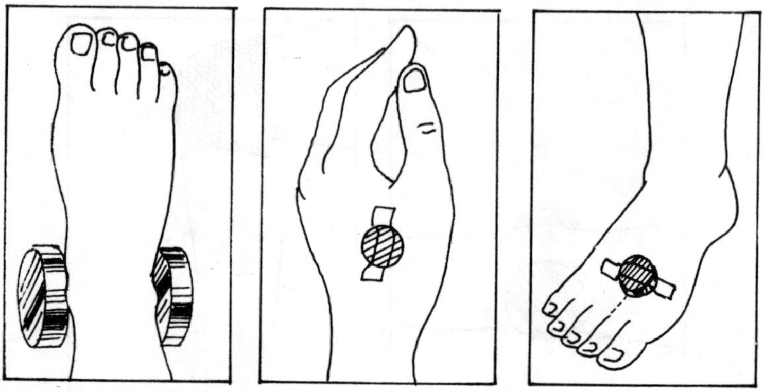

**Magnetic treatment :** (1) The **north pole** of a strong magnet should be applied to one side and the **south pole** to the other side of the affected joint, for 15-30 minutes, 2-3 times a day. (2) The **north pole** of a small magnet should be stuck to the muscular prominence between the thumb and the first finger. (3) The **north pole** of another small magnet should be stuck to the web between the second toe (the one adjacent to the big toe) and the third toe.

**(12) Foot or heel pain :**

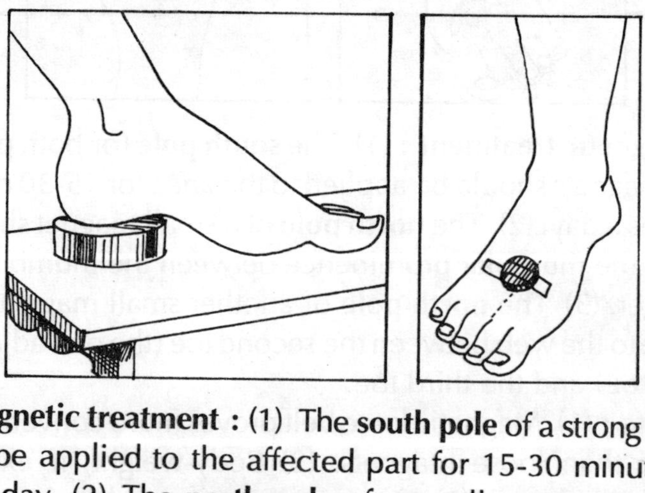

**Magnetic treatment :** (1) The **south pole** of a strong magnet should be applied to the affected part for 15-30 minutes, 2-3 times a day. (2) The **north pole** of a small magnet should be stuck to the web between the second toe (the one adjacent to the big toe) and the third toe.

**(13) Abdominal pain :**

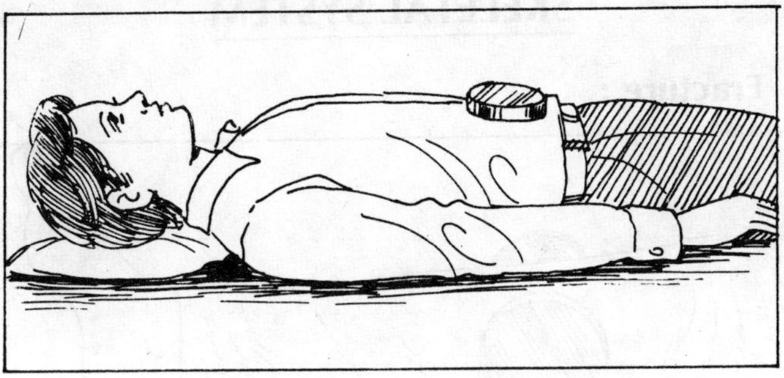

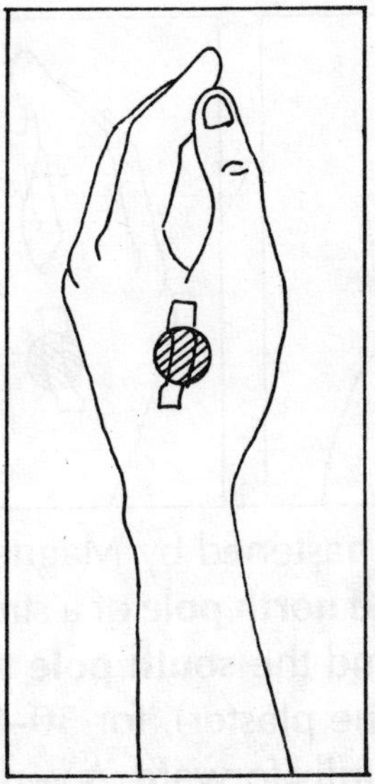

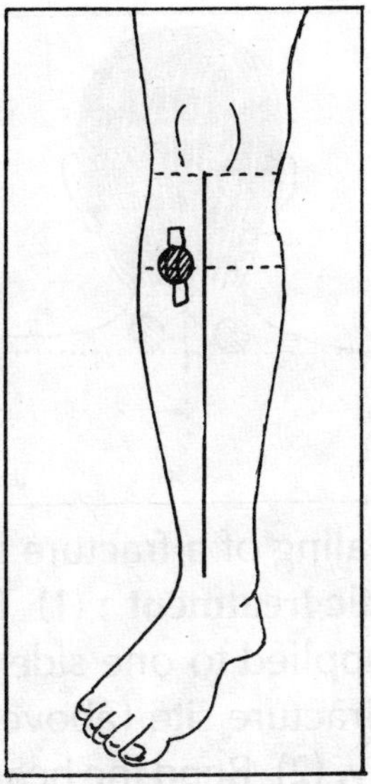

**Magnetic treatment :** (1) The **south pole** of a strong magnet should be applied to the paining part for 15-30 minutes, 2-3 times a day. (2) The **north pole** of a small magnet should be stuck to the muscular prominence between the thumb and the first finger. (3) The **north pole** of another small magnet should be stuck to a point which is four finger-breaths below the lower border of the round knee-bone (see the figure). (4) Magnetised water should be drunk 4-5 times a day.

**Note :** If pain is severe, fomentation with a hot waterbag may help.

# 18. DISORDERS OF THE MUSCULO-SKELETAL SYSTEM

**(1) Fracture :**

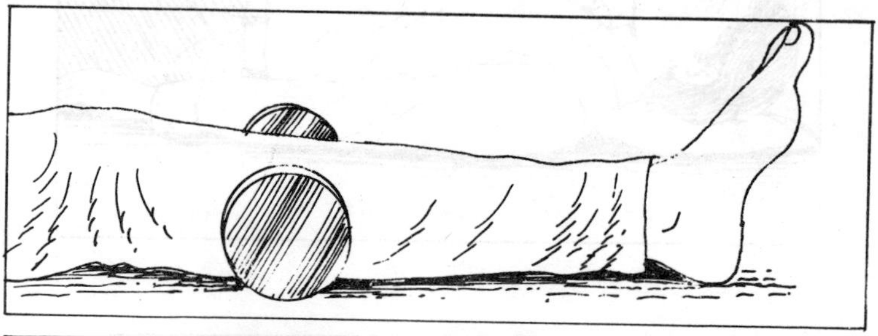

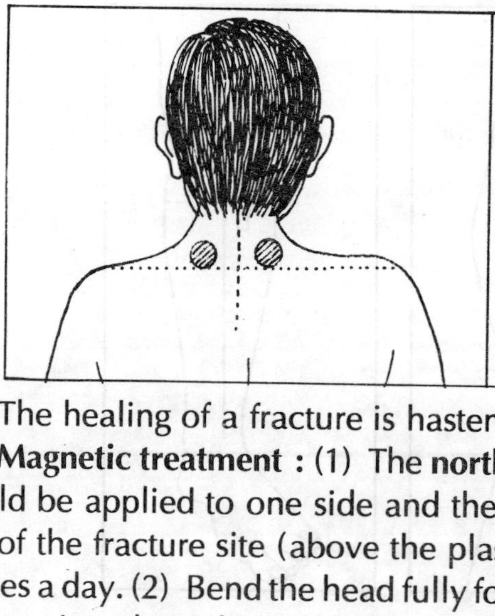

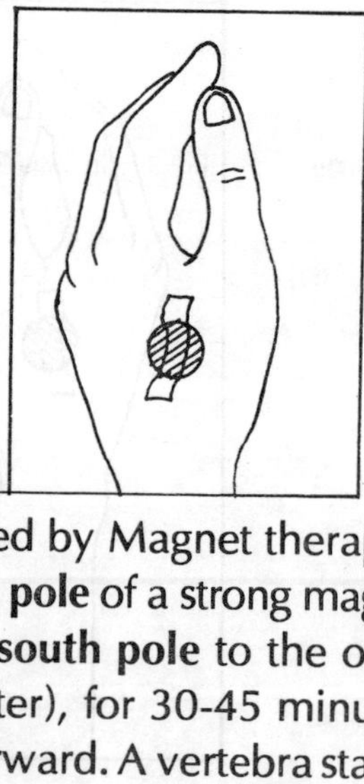

The healing of a fracture is hastened by Magnet therapy.

**Magnetic treatment :** (1) The **north pole** of a strong magnet should be applied to one side and the **south pole** to the other side of the fracture site (above the plaster), for 30-45 minutes, 2 times a day. (2) Bend the head fully forward. A vertebra stands out prominently on the neck. This is called $C_7$ vertebra. The next lower vertebra is called the $T_1$ vertebra. Stick the **north poles** of two small magnets, one-one inch to the either side of $T_1$ vertebra. (3) If there is pain, the **north pole** of a small magnet should be stuck to the muscular prominence between the thumb and the first finger. (4) Magnetised water should be drunk 4-5 times a day.

**(2) Sciatica; Lumbago :** (see backache)

**(3) Cervical spondylosis :** (see neck pain)

**(4) Osteoarthritis of the knee :** (see knee pain)

**(5) Frozen shoulder; Periarthritis of the shoulder :** (see shoulder pain)

**(6) Tennis elbow (muscular pain at the outer edge of the elbow) :**

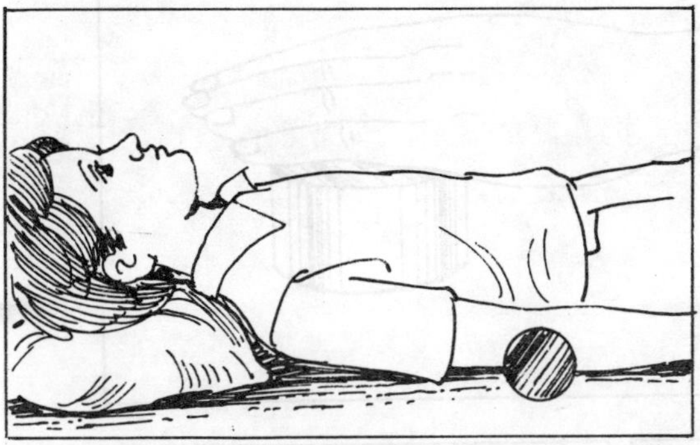

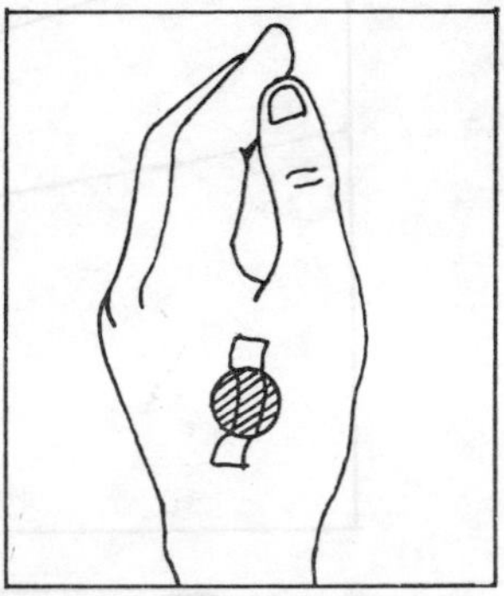

**Magnetic treatment :** (1) The **south pole** of a strong magnet should be applied to the paining part for 15-20 minutes, 2-3 times a day. (2) The **north pole** of small magnet should be stuck to the muscular prominence between the thumb and the first finger.

**(7) Gout :**

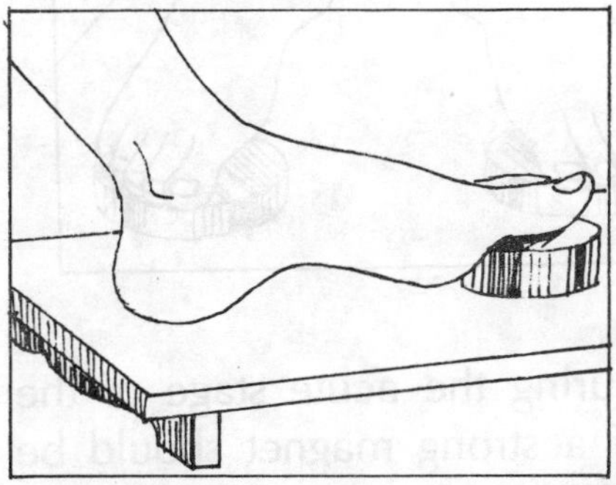

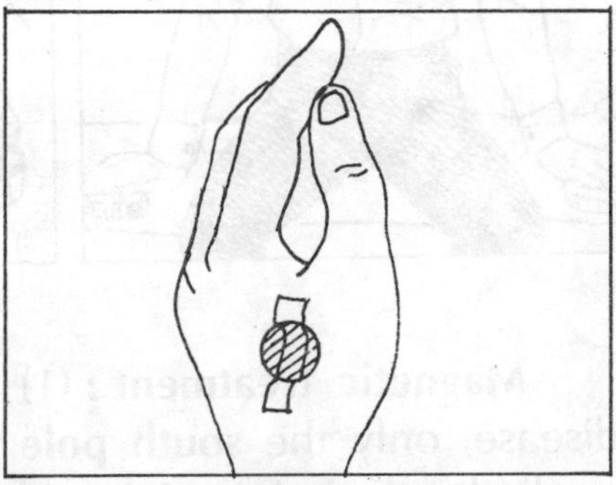

**Magnetic treatment :** (1) The **south pole** of a strong magnet should be applied to the paining part for 30-45 minutes, 2-3 times a day. (2) The **north pole** of a small magnet should be stuck to the muscular prominence between the thumb and the first finger. (3) Magnetised water should be drunk 4-5 times a day.

**Note :** Bread, meat, fish, alcohol or any other food which has been found to precipitate attacks of this disease should be strictly avoided.

## (8) Rheumatoid Arthritis :

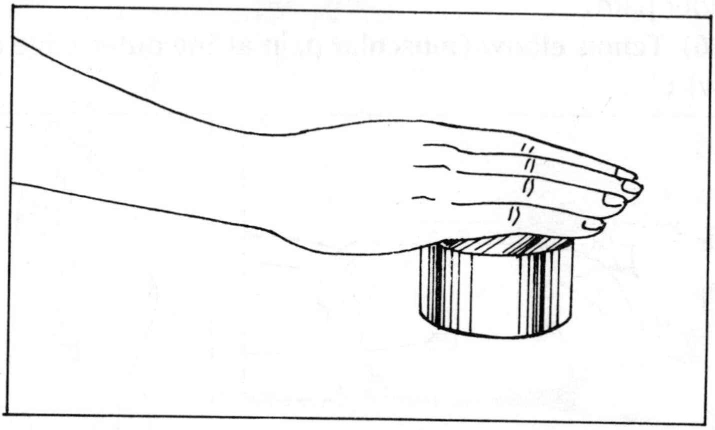

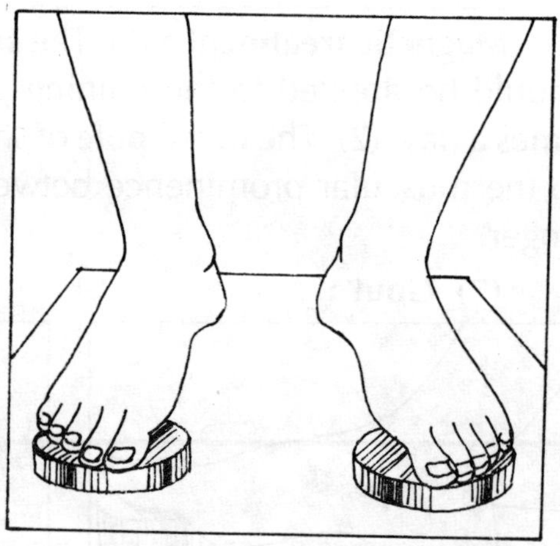

**Magnetic treatment :** (1) During the acute stage of the disease, only the **south pole** of a strong magnet should be applied to the paining joint, for 15-45 minutes, 2-3 times a day; during remissions (or if the disease is mild) both the poles can be simultaneously used instead of the **south pole** alone. (2) Right palm should be kept in contact with the **north pole** and the left palm should be kept in contact with the **south pole** of strong magnets for 15 minutes, once or twice daily. Soles of the feet, too, can be similarly treated. Such treatment of the palms and the soles is found to give good benefits to a number of patients. (3) Magnetised water should be drunk 4-5 times a day.

## (9) Muscle weakness or Muscle diseases (Myopathies) :

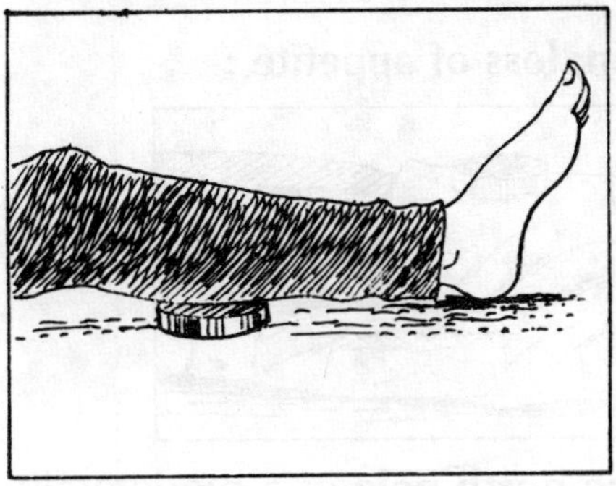

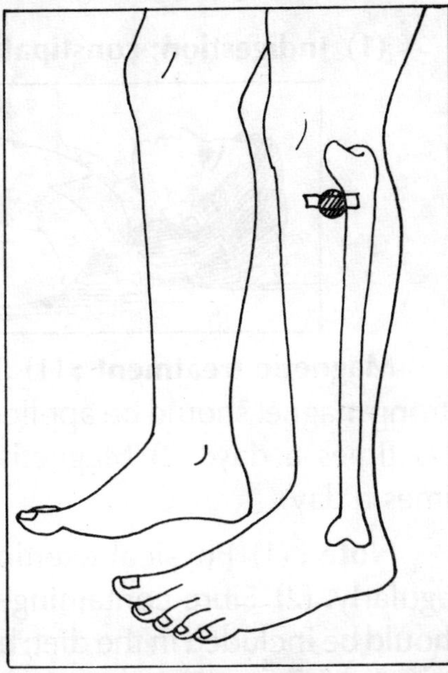

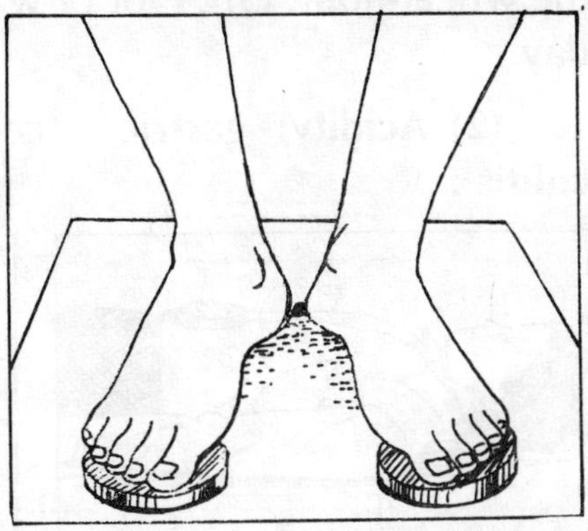

**Magnetic treatment :** (1) The **north pole** of a strong magnet should be applied to the weak muscles, for 30-45 minutes, 2-3 times a day. (2) On the outer aspect of the leg, just below the knee joint, a prominent bone (the head of the fibula) can be seen. The **north pole** of a small magnet should be stuck exactly below this prominent bone. (3) Left palm (or sole) and right palm (or sole) can be kept in contact with the **north** and the **south poles**, respectively, of strong magnets for 15-20 minutes, once or twice a day.

# 19. DISORDERS OF THE DIGESTIVE SYSTEM

**(1) Indigestion; constipation; loss of appetite :**

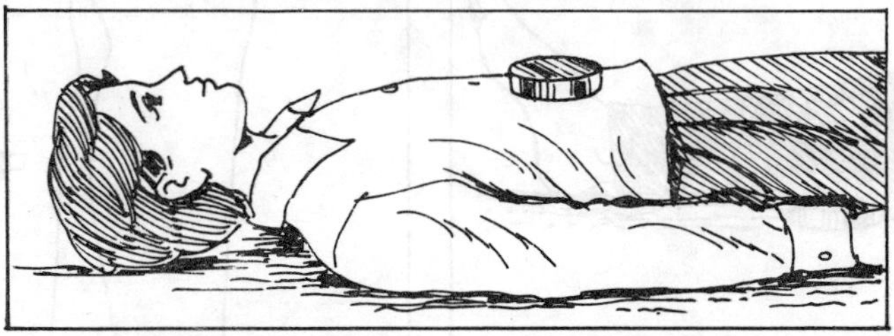

**Magnetic treatment :** (1) The **north pole** of a moderately strong magnet should be applied to the navel for 15-30 minutes, 2-3 times a day. (2) Magnetised water should be drunk 4-5 times a day.

**Note :** (1) Physical exertion or exercises should be done regularly. (2) Fibre-containing foods like fruits and vegetables should be included in the diet; bran should not be removed from the wheat-flour. (3) A lot of water should be drunk during the day.

**(2) Acidity; gastric ulcer; abdominal pain; dysentry; colitis :**

**Magnetic treatment :** (1) The **south pole** of a moderately strong magnet should be applied to the navel for 15-30 minutes, 2-3 times a day. (2) Water magnetised with the **south pole** alone should be drunk 4-5 times a day. (3) Persons with hyperacidity or gastric ulcer should apply the **south pole** of a weak magnet to the forehead for 15 minutes, twice a day.

**Note :** (1) Simple, bland diet should be taken. (2) The cause for mental tension should be sought for and eliminated.

**(3) Appendicitis :**

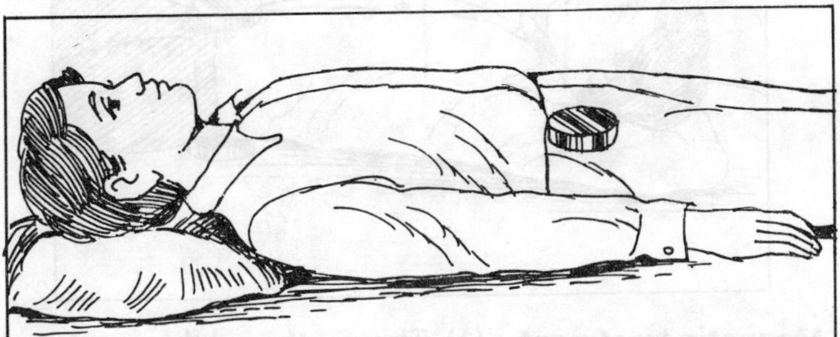

**Magnetic treatment :** (1) The **south pole** of a strong magnet should be applied to the paining spot for 30-45 minutes, 2-3 times a day. (2) Magnetised water should be drunk 4-5 times a day.

**(4) Nausea-Vomitting :**

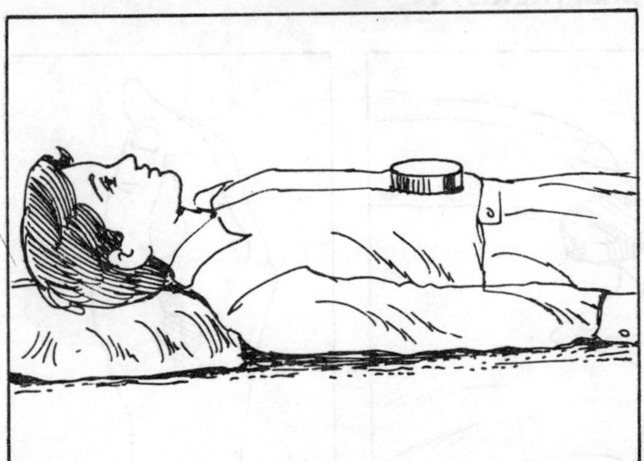

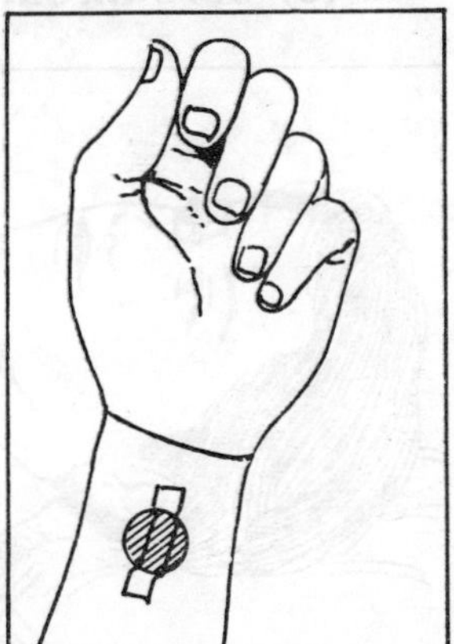

**Magnetic treatment :** (1) The **south pole** of a moderately strong magnet should be applied to the upper abdomen whenever needed (or 2-3 times a day) for 15-30 minutes. (2) Water magnetised with both the poles (or only the **south pole**) should be drunk 4-5 times a day. (3) The **north pole** of a small magnet should be stuck to the middle of the wrist, three finger-breadths above the wrist-crease (see the figure).

**(5) Jaundice; liver ailments :**

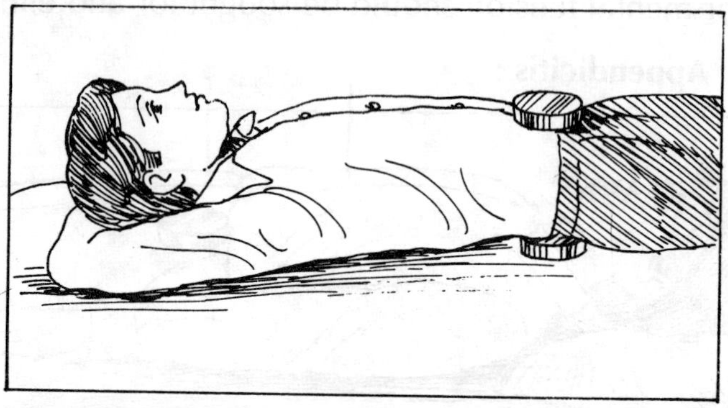

**Magnetic treatment :** (1) The **north** and the **south poles** of strong magnets should be simultaneously applied to the right side of the abdomen (on the liver area) for 15-30 minutes, 4-5 times a day; however, if the liver has been enlarged or is painful, only the **south pole** should be used. (2) Magnetised water should be drunk 4-5 times a day.

**(6) Sore throat (pharyngitis) :**

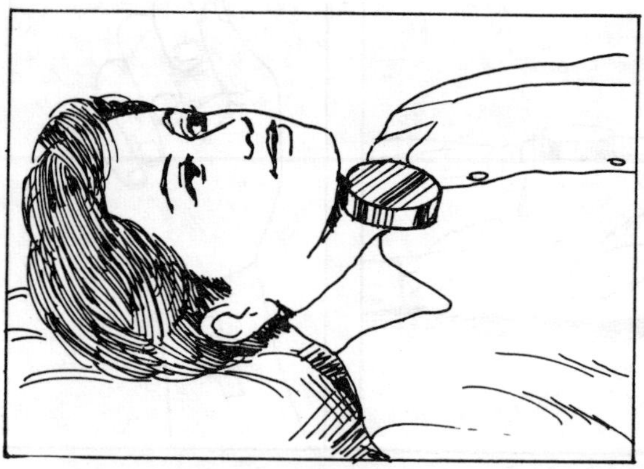

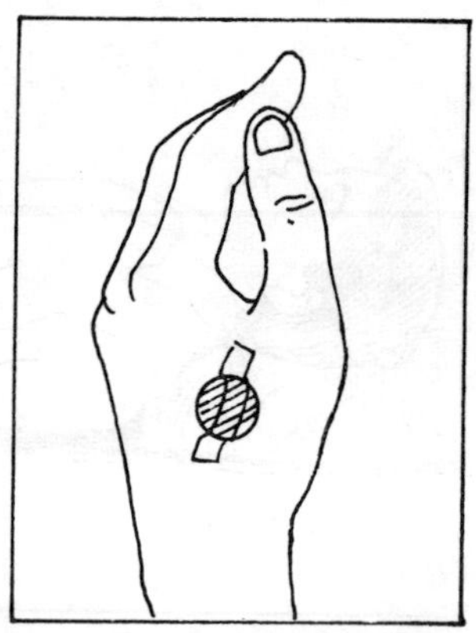

**Magnetic treatment :** (1) The **south pole** of a moderately strong magnet should be applied to the throat for 15-30 minutes, 2-3 times a day. (2) Gargles should be done with water magnetised by the **south pole.** (3) Magnetised water should be drunk 4-5 times a day. (4) The **north pole** of a small magnet should be stuck to the muscular prominence between the thumb and the first finger.

**(7) Piles; anal fissures; anal fistula :**

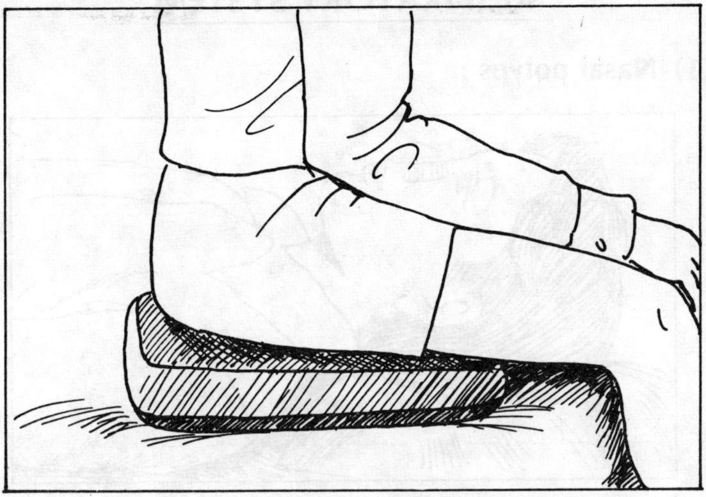

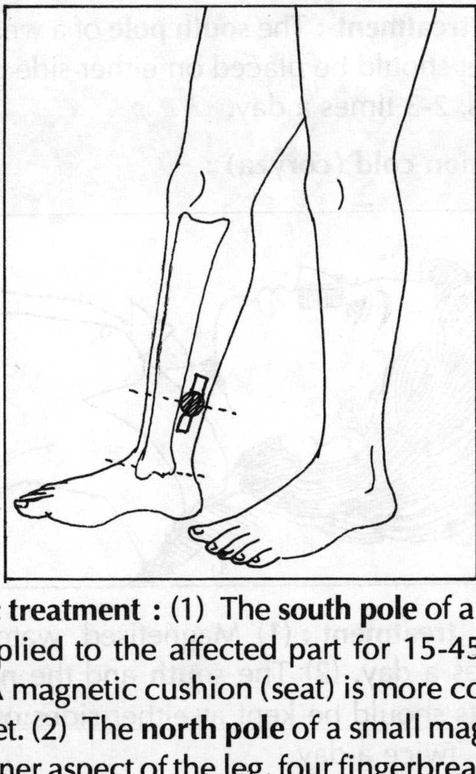

**Magnetic treatment :** (1) The **south pole** of a strong magnet should be applied to the affected part for 15-45 minutes, 2-3 times a day. A magnetic cushion (seat) is more convenient than a loose magnet. (2) The **north pole** of a small magnet should be stuck to the inner aspect of the leg, four fingerbreadths above the inner prominence of the ankle bone. (3) Magnetised water should be drunk 4-5 times a day.

**Note :** Constipation should be strictly avoided.

# 20. DISORDERS OF THE RESPIRATORY SYSTEM

**(1) Nasal polyps :**

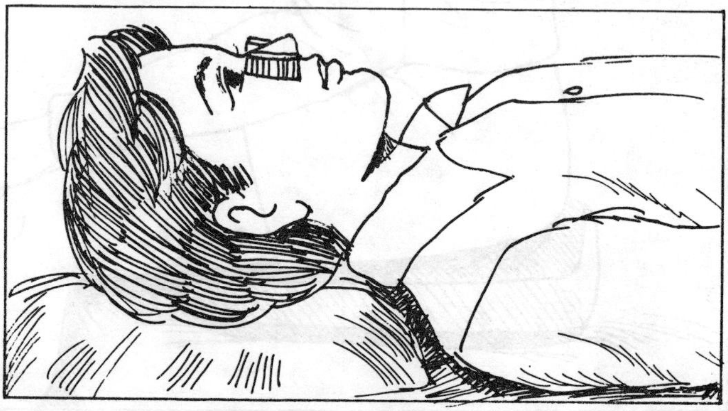

**Magnetic treatment :** The **south pole** of a weak (or medium power) magnet should be placed on either side of the nose for 15-30 minutes, 2-3 times a day.

**(2) Common cold (coryza) :**

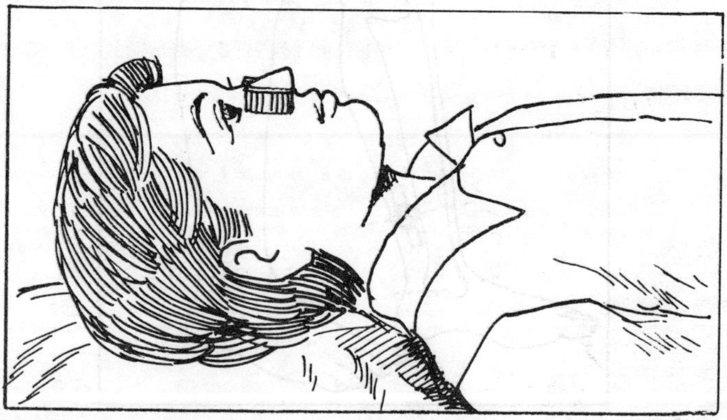

**Magnetic treatment :** (1) Magnetised water should be drunk 4-5 times a day. (2) The **south** and the **north poles** of curved magnets should be kept at either sides of the nose for 10-15 minutes, twice a day.

**Note :** Cold eatables and drinks should be avoided. Inhalation of steam also helps.

**(3) Tonsillitis :**

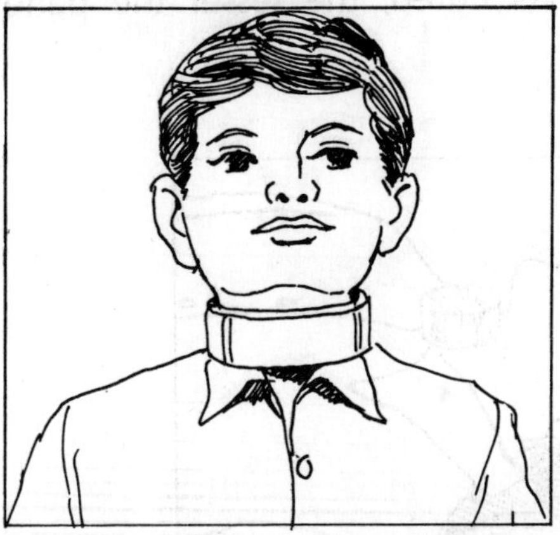

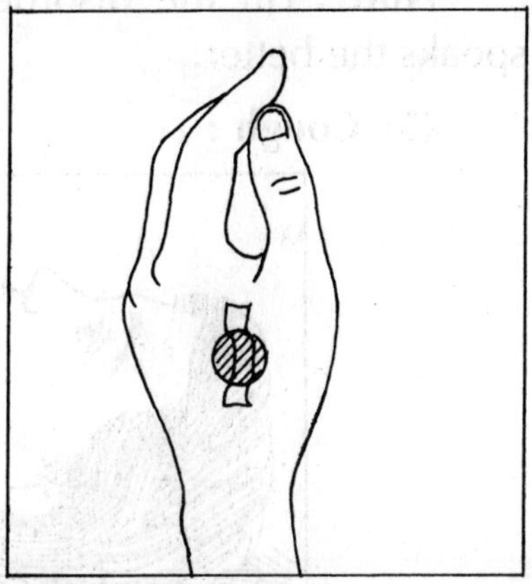

**Magnetic treatment :** (1) The **south poles** of moderately strong magnets should be applied below the lower jaw, on the tonsillar area, for 15-30 minutes, 2-3 times a day. (2) Magnetised water should be drunk 4-5 times a day. (3) Gargling should be done with water magnetised with the **south pole.** (4) If there is pain in the throat or if swallowing is difficult, the **north pole** of small magnet should be stuck (with sticking plaster) to the muscular prominence between the thumb and the first finger.

**(4) Hoarseness or loss of voice; Laryngitis :**

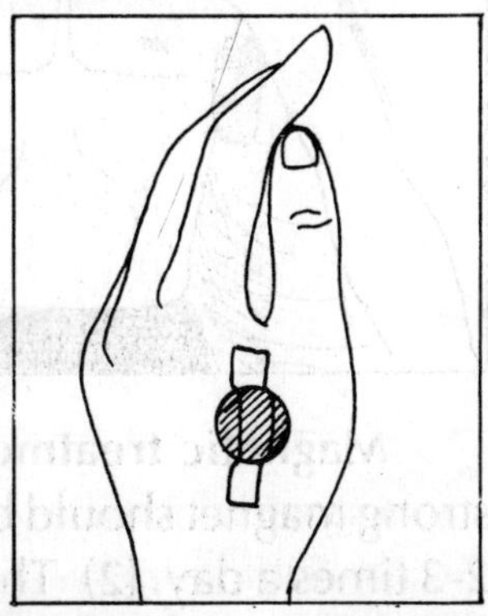

**Magnetic treatment :** (1) The **south pole** of a moderately strong magnet should be applied on the throat, for 15-30 minutes, 2-3 times a day. (2) Magnetised water should be drunk 4-5 times a day. (3) The **north pole** of a small magnet should be stuck to muscular prominence between thumb and first finger.

**Note :** Till the disorder is cured, the lesser the patient speaks the better.

**(5) Cough :**

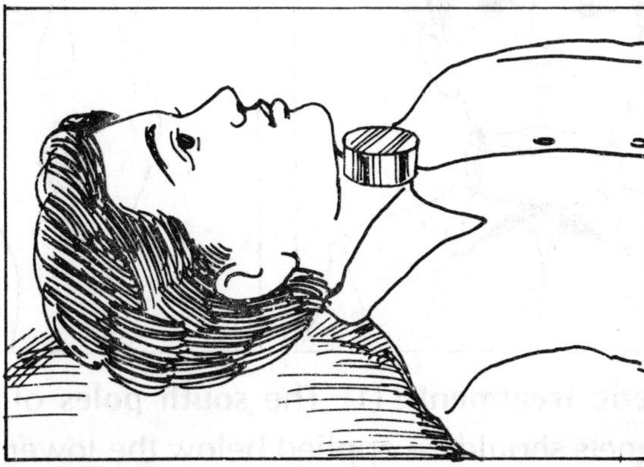

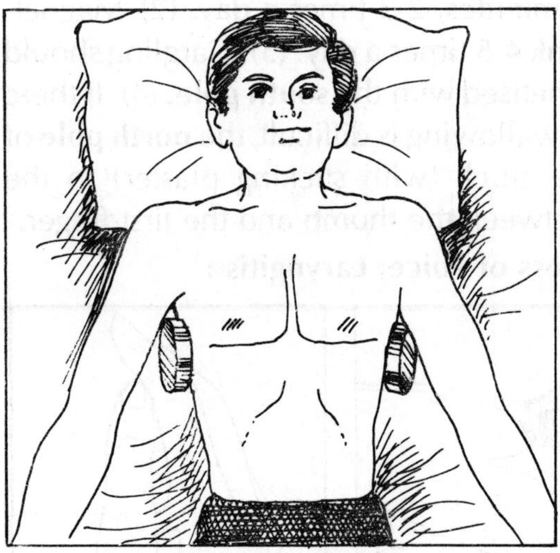

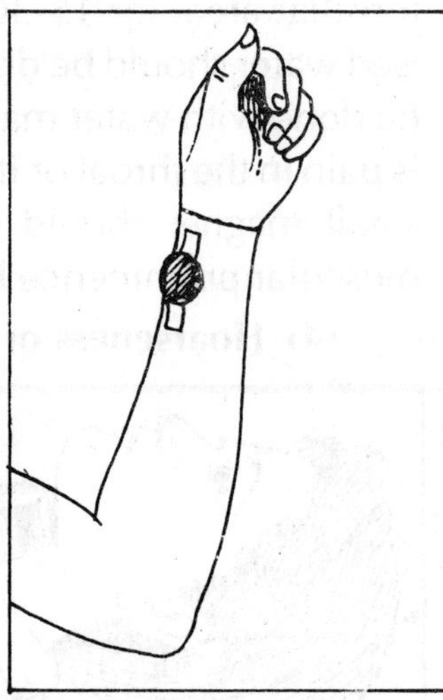

**Magnetic treatment :** (1) The **south pole** of a moderately strong magnet should be applied to the throat for 15-30 minutes, 2-3 times a day. (2) The **south pole** of a strong magnet should be placed on one side and the **north pole** on the other side of the chest, for 15-30 minutes, 2-3 times a day. (3) Magnetised water should be drunk 4-5 times a day. (4) The **north pole** of a small magnet should be stuck to the outer (thumb side) edge of the wrist, one inch away from the base of the palm.

## (6) Asthma :

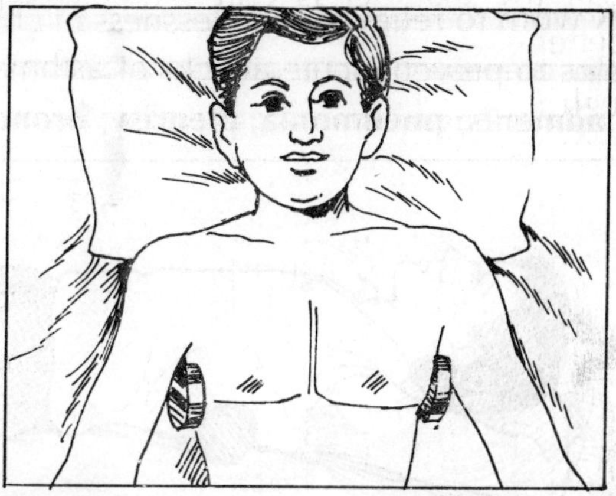

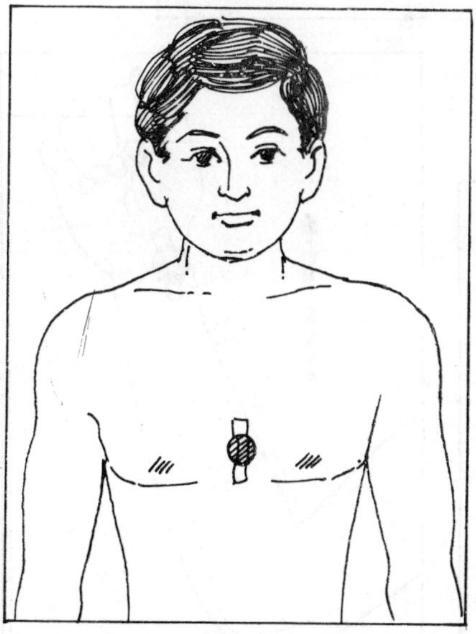

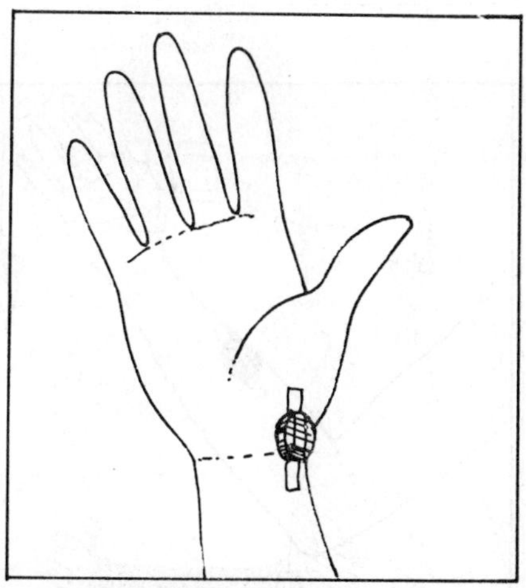

**Magnetic treatment :** (1) The **south pole** of a strong magnet should be applied on one side and the **north pole** on the other side of the chest for 30-45 minutes, 2-3 times a day. (2) The **north pole** of a small magnet should be stuck on the chest, on the mid-point of an imaginary line joining the two nipples. (3) The **north pole** of a small magnet should be stuck to the outer (thumb) end of wrist crease. (4) Magnetised water should be drunk 4-5 times a day.

**Note :** (1) Magnetic chest belt can be worn to relieve an acute attack of asthma. (2) Magnetic necklace may be continuously worn to relieve breathlessness of chronic asthma. This also helps to prevent acute attacks of asthma.

(7) **Lung ailments; pneumonia; pleurisy; bronchitis :**

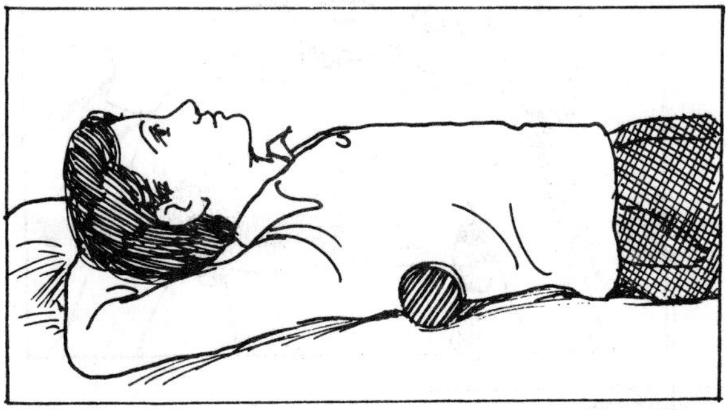

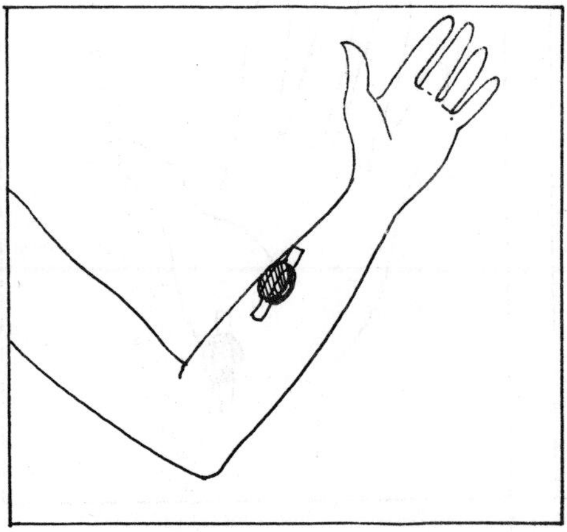

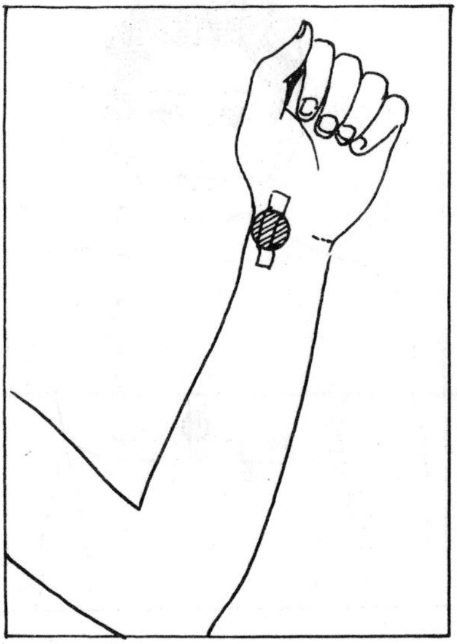

**Magnetic treatment** : (1) The **south pole** of a strong magnet should be applied to the affected part of the chest, for 30-45 minutes, 2-3 times a day. (2) If the disease is acute, the **north pole** of a small magnet should be stuck to the outer (thumb side) edge of the forearm, midway between the wrist and the elbow. However, if the disease is of a chronic nature, the **north pole** of a small magnet should be stuck to the outer edge of the wrist joint, in line with the thumb. (3) Magnetised water should be drunk 4-5 times a day.

## 21. DISORDERS OF THE HEART AND BLOOD VESSELS

### (1) High blood pressure (Hypertension) :

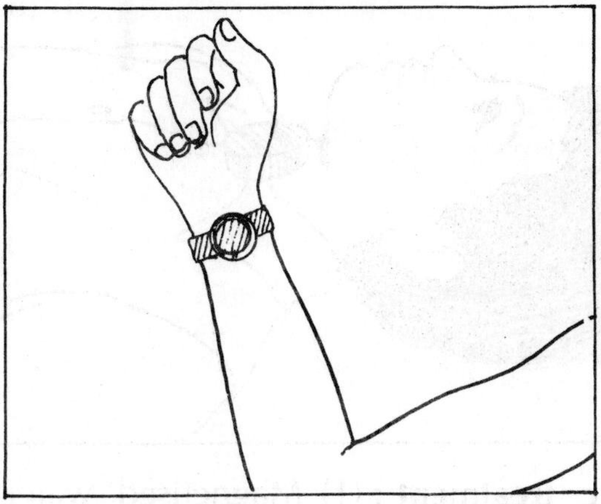

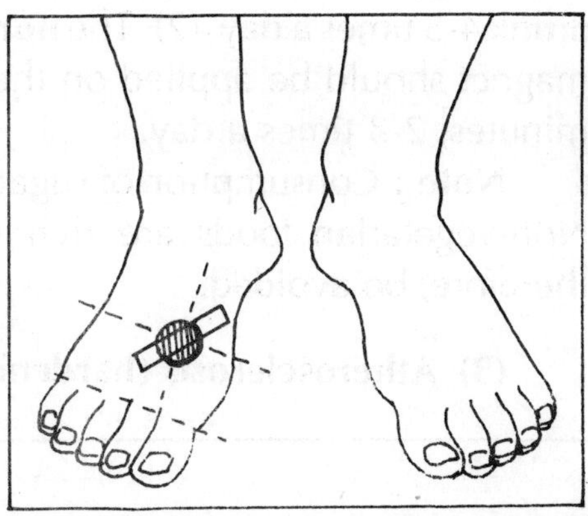

**Magnetic treatment :** (1) The magnetic wrist belt should be continuously worn on the right wrist. (2) The **south pole** of a weak magnet should be applied to the forehead for 15-30 minutes, 2-3 times a day. (3) The **north pole** of a small magnet should be stuck to the web between the great toe and the first toe of the foot. (4) Magnetised water should be drunk 4-5 times a day.

**Note :** Shavasana should be done for 10-15 minutes, twice a day. Dietary changes should be brought about, the intake of salt and fats should be curtailed.

**(2) Hypercholesterolaemia (high cholesterol level in the blood) :**

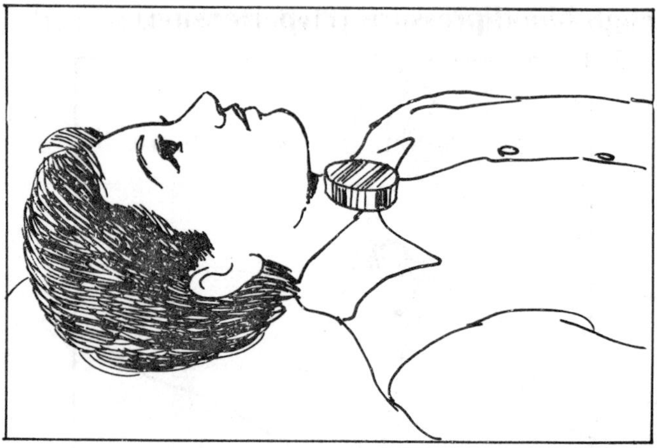

**Magnetic treatment :** (1) Magnetised water should be drunk 4-5 times a day. (2) The **north pole** of a moderately strong magnet should be applied on the base of the throat for 15-30 minutes, 2-3 times a day.

**Note :** Consumption of sugar and fats should be cut down. Non-vegetarian foods are rich in cholesterol. They should, therefore, be avoided.

**(3) Atherosclerosis (hardening of the blood vessels) :**

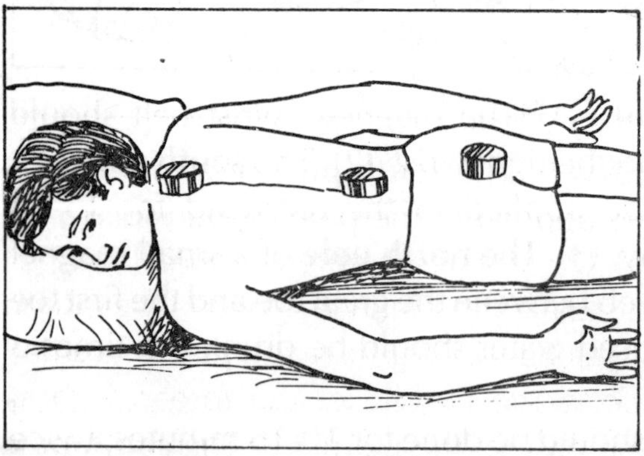

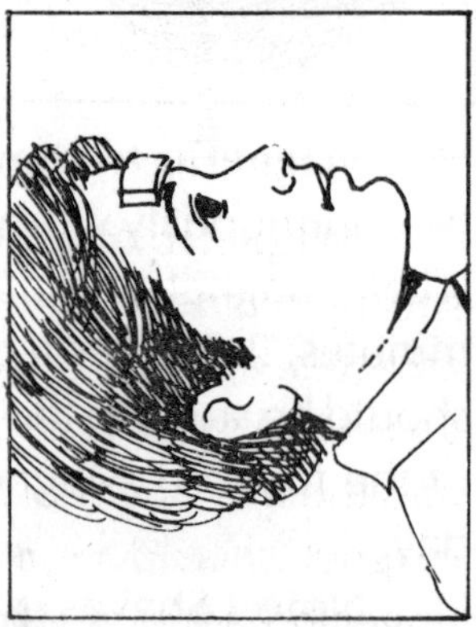

**Magnetic treatment :** (1) Magnetised water should be drunk 4-5 times a day. (2) The **north poles** of strong magnets should be placed on three parts of the spine : at the base of the neck, parallel to the navel and at the lower end of the spine, for 15-30 minutes, once or twice a day. (3) The **south pole** of a weak magnet should be applied to the forehead for 15-30 minutes, 2-3 times a day.

**(4) Chest pain (angina pectoris); Palpitation :**

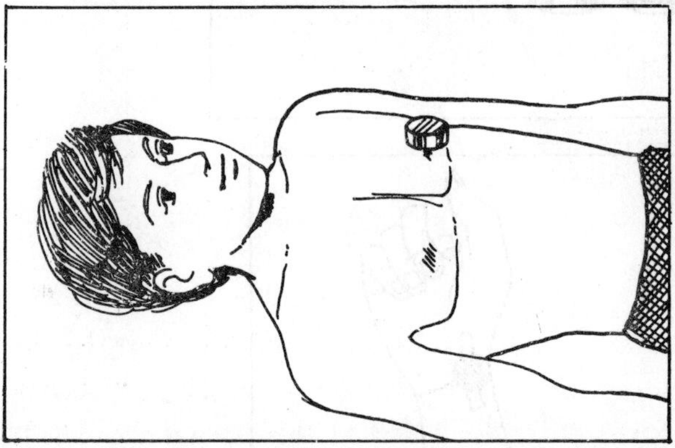

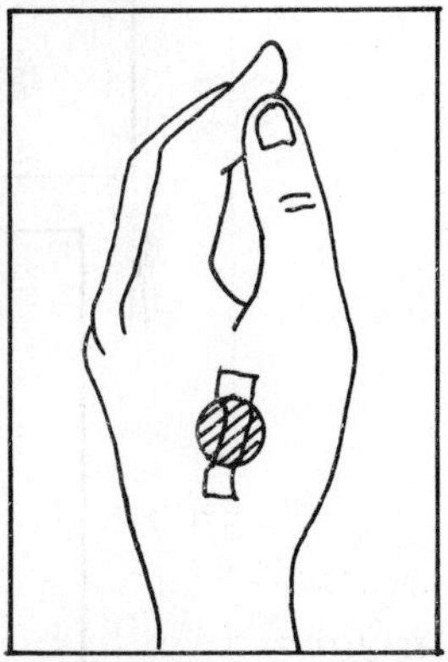

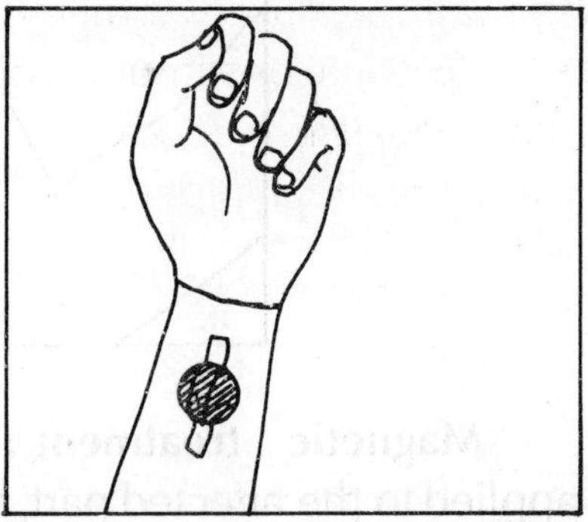

**Magnetic treatment** : (1) The **south pole** of a moderately strong magnet should be applied to the paining part for 15-45 minutes, as per the need. (2) The **north pole** of a small magnet should be stuck to the muscular prominence between the thumb and the first finger of the left hand. (3) The **north pole** of a small magnet should be stuck to the middle of the forearm, three finger-breadths above the base of the palm. (4) The **south pole** of a weak magnet should be applied to the forehead for 15-45 minutes. (5) Magnetised water should be drunk.

**Note** : Till the pain subsides, complete bed-rest is essential.

**(5) Varicose veins :**

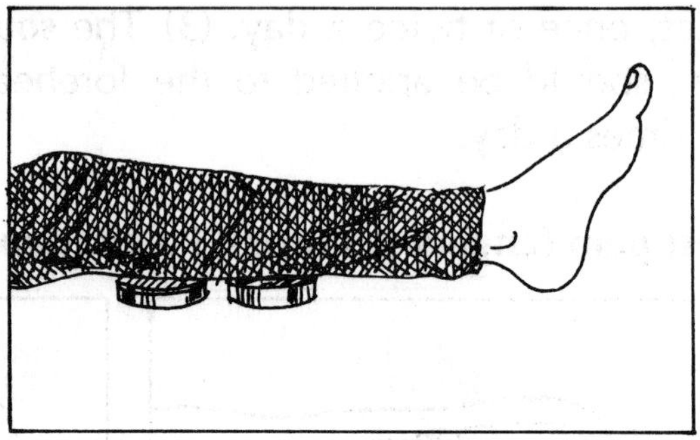

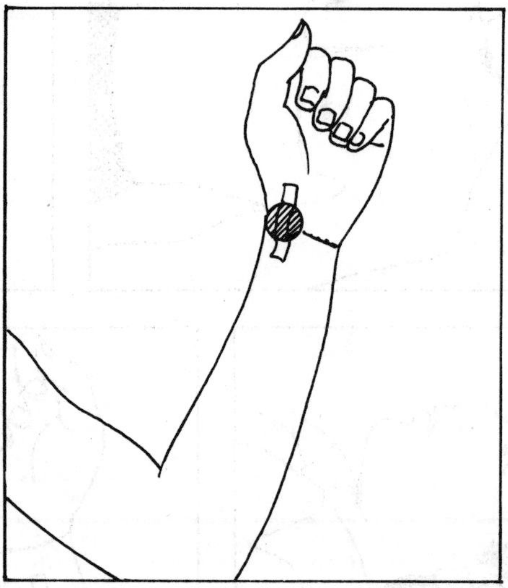

**Magnetic treatment :** (1) Strong magnets should be applied to the affected part, with the **north pole** on the one side and the **south pole** on the other, for 15-45 minutes, 2-3 times a day. (2) The **north pole** of a small magnet should be stuck to the outer edge of the palm crease, in line with the thumb. (3) Magnetised water should be drunk 4-5 times a day.

**Note :** That part of the body which bears varicose veins should be kept elevated for 10-15 minutes every day and exercises of that part should be performed, e.g. if there are varicose veins in the calf, the entire leg should be kept elevated with the help of pillows or a sofa and the foot should be moved in different directions.

# 22. DISORDERS OF THE NERVOUS SYSTEM

**(1) Chorea (tremors, rhythmic unsteadiness of bodyparts) :**

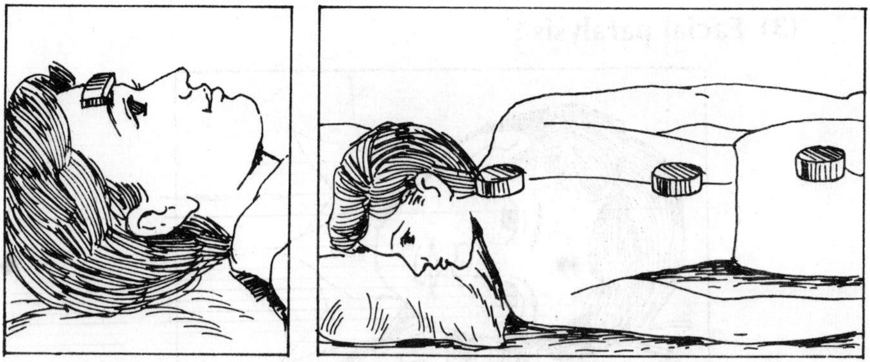

**Magnetic treatment :** (1) The **south pole** of a weak magnet should be applied to the forehead for 15-45 minutes, 2-3 times a day. (2) The **north poles** of strong magnets should be placed on three parts of the vertebral column, at the base of the neck, parallel to the navel and at the lower end of the spine, for 15-30 minutes, 2-3 times a day. (3) Magnetised water should be drunk 4-5 times a day.

**(2) Convulsions :**

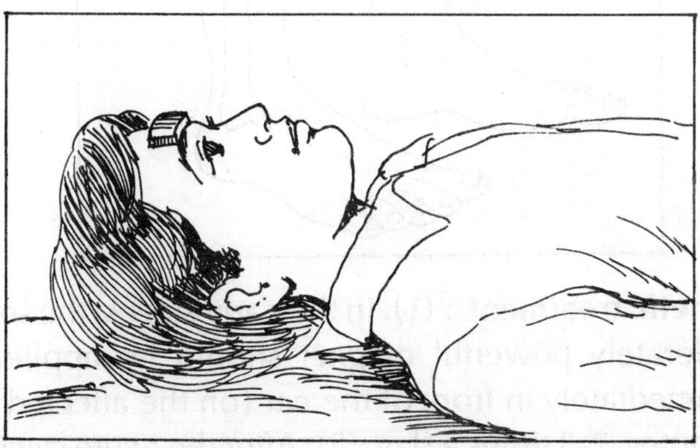

**Magnetic treatment :** (1) During a fit of convulsions, the **south pole** of a weak magnet should be kept on the forehead, for the required time. (2) Between two attacks, the **south pole** of a weak magnet should be placed on the forehead for 15-20 minutes, 2-3 times a day. (3) Magnetised water should be drunk 4-5 times a day.

**(3) Facial paralysis :**

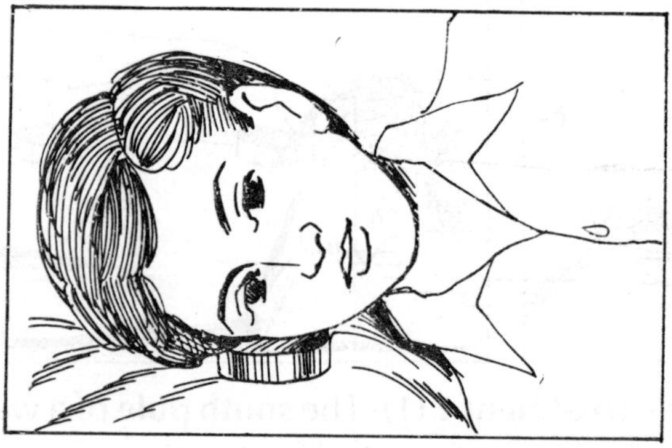

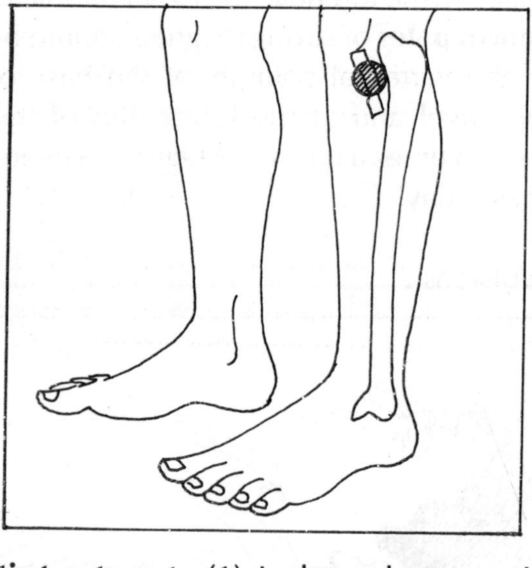

**Magnetic treatment :** (1) In the early stages, the **south pole** of a moderately powerful magnet should be applied to the cheek, immediately in front of the ear (on the affected side) for 15-20 minutes, 2-3 times a day. (2) After the acute stage is over, the **north pole** of a medium power magnet should be applied in front of the ear for 15-20 minutes, 2-3 times a day. (3) The **north pole** of a small magnet should be stuck below the knee, on the outer aspect of the leg, just below the prominently seen bone.

**(4) Poliomyelitis :**

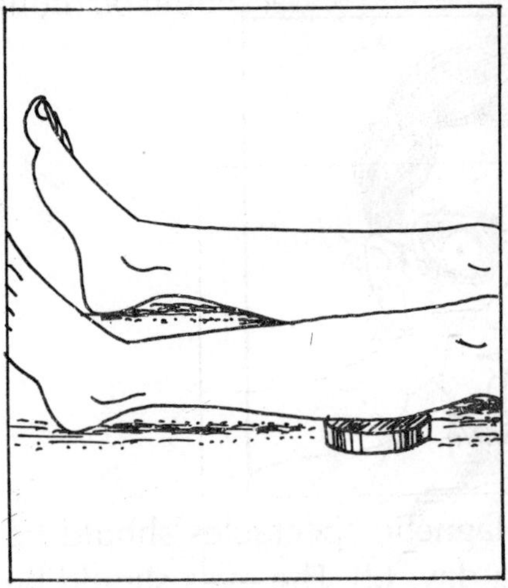

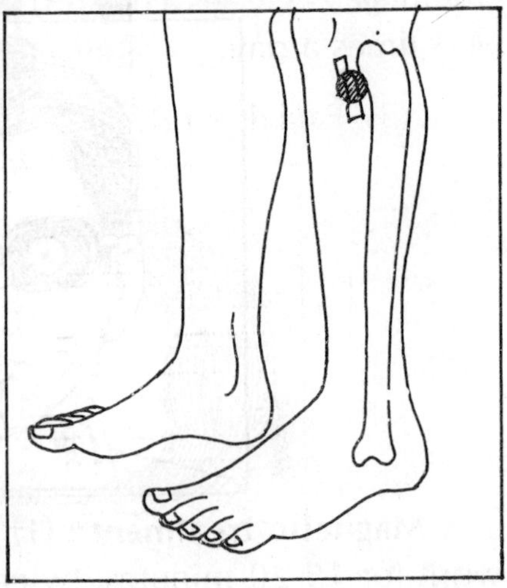

**Magnetic treatment** : (1) In the acute stage, there is severe pain in the affected muscles. Hence the south pole of a strong magnet should be applied to the affected muscles for 15-20 minutes, 2-3 times a day. (2) Once the acute stage is over, the **north pole** of a strong magnet should be applied to the affected muscles for 30-45 minutes, 2-3 times a day. This would give strength to the muscles and hasten recovery. (3) The **north pole** of a small magnet should be stuck to the outer aspect of the leg, just below the knee, just below the prominently seen bone. (4) Magnetised water should be drunk 4-5 times a day.

## 23. DISORDERS OF THE SENSE ORGANS

**(1) Eye ailments :**

**Magnetic treatment :** (1) Magnetic spectacles should be worn for 15-20 minutes, twice a day. (2) The eyes should be washed, by immersing them in magnetised water for a minute or two.

**Note :** For refractive errors (numbers) and squint, eye exercises are indispensable. Details about these have been presented in the book 'Care of the Eyes', and 'Vision Training Programme' by the same authors.

**(2) Ear ailments :**

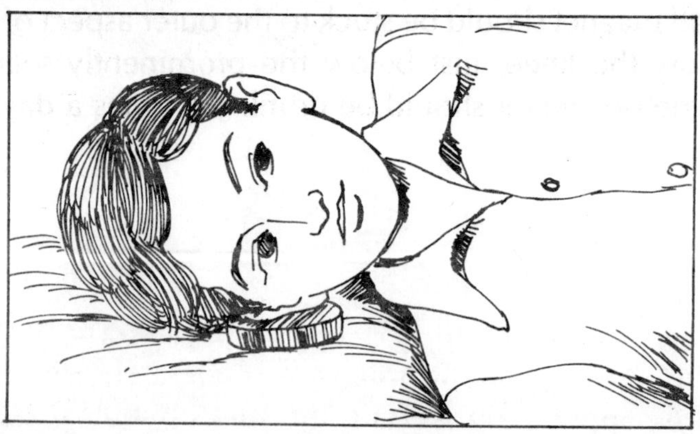

**Magnetic treatment :** (1) If there is pain in or pus-discharge from the ear, the **south pole** of a moderately strong magnet should be applied to the ear for 15-30 minutes, 2-3

times a day. However, in case of deafness, the **north pole** should be used instead of the **south pole.** (2) Magnetised oil should be dropped into the ear once or twice a day.

**(3) Nose ailments :**

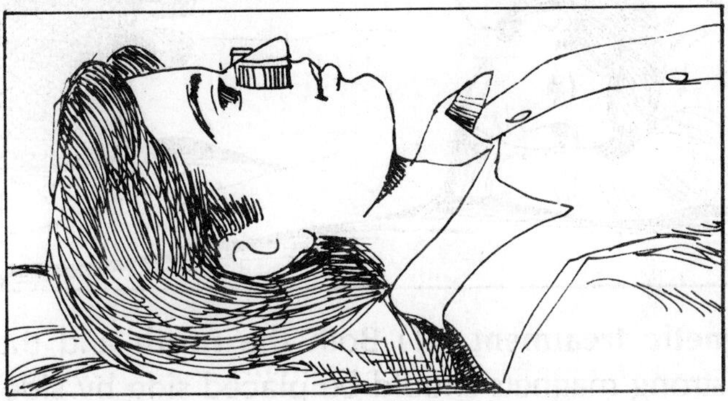

**Magnetic treatment :** The **south pole** of a weak magnet (preferably rectangular or crescent shaped) should be applied to one side of the nose and the **north pole** to the other side, for 15-30 minutes, 2-3 times a day.

**(4) Skin ailments :**

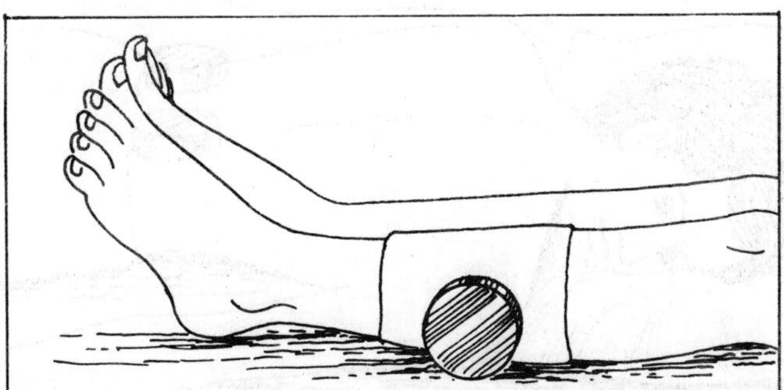

**Magnetic treatment :** (1) If there is itching of or discharge from the skin, the **south pole** of a moderately strong magnet should be applied to that part, for 30-45 minutes, 2-3 times a day. It is desirable to interpose a thin cloth between the skin and the magnet. However, in case of white spots on the skin (leucoderma), the **north pole** should be used instead of the **south pole.** (2) Magnetised water should be drunk 4-5 times a day.

## 24. DISORDERS OF THE URINARY SYSTEM

### (1) Kidney-stone :

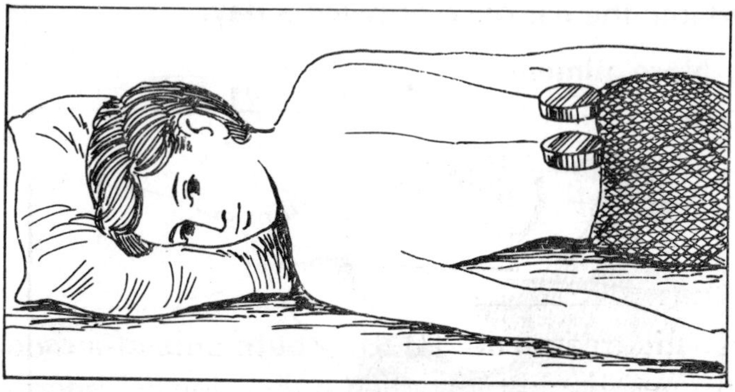

**Magnetic treatment :** (1) Both the **north** and the **south poles** of strong magnets should be placed side by side on the lower part of the back for 30-45 minutes, 2-3 times a day. A magnetic waist belt proves more convenient and effective. (2) Magnetised water should be drunk 4-5 times a day.

### (2) Kidney-ailments :

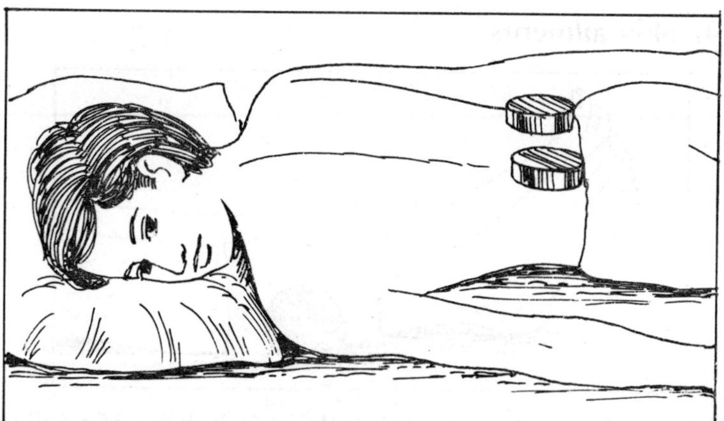

**Magnetic treatment** : (1) The **south pole** of a strong magnet should be applied to the lower back for 30-45 minutes, 2-3 times a day. If infection has been ruled out, both the poles can be simultaneously used instead of the **south pole** alone. (2) Magnetised water should be drunk 4-5 times a day.

**(3) Ailments of the urinary bladder :**

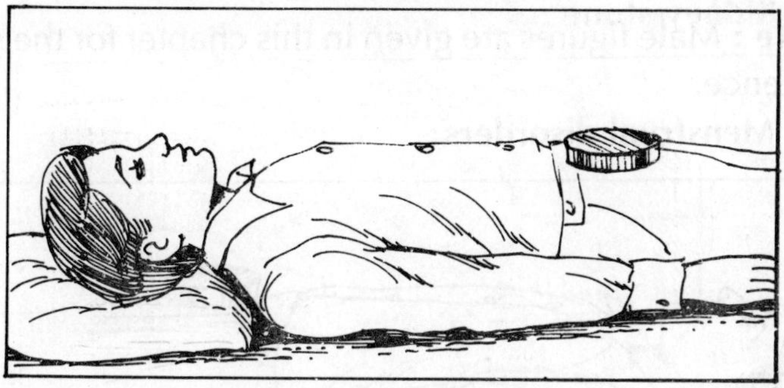

**Magnetic treatment :** (1) The **south pole** of a moderately strong magnet should be applied on the lower abdomen, just above the genitals, for 15-30 minutes, 2-3 times a day. (2) Magnetised water should be drunk 4-5 times a day.

# 25. DISORDERS OF THE REPRODUCTIVE SYSTEM

**Note :** Male figures are given in this chapter for the sake of convenience.

**(1) Menstrual disorders :**

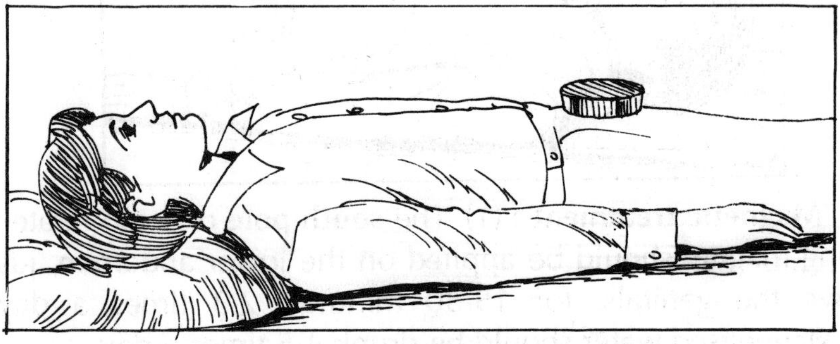

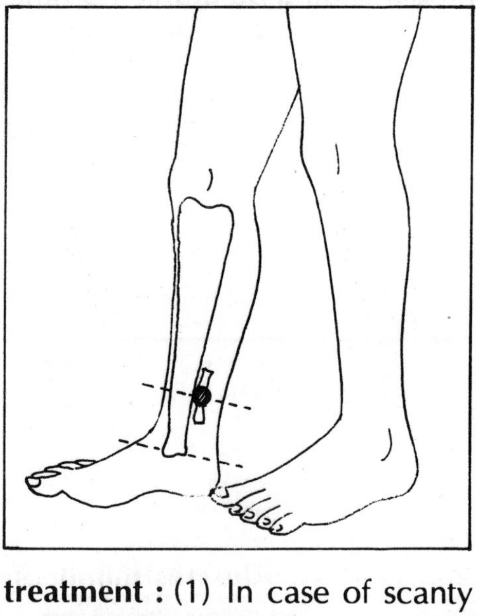

**Magnetic treatment :** (1) In case of scanty menstruation, the **north pole** and in case of excessive or painful menstruation, the **south pole** of a medium power or strong magnet should be applied to the perineum (the part between the genitals and the anus) for 15-30 minutes, 2-3 times a day. (2) The **north pole** of a small magnet should be stuck to the inner aspect of the leg, four finger-breadths above the inner prominence of the ankle bone. (3) Magnetised water should be drunk 4-5 times a day.

## (2) Sexual debility; impotence; frigidity :

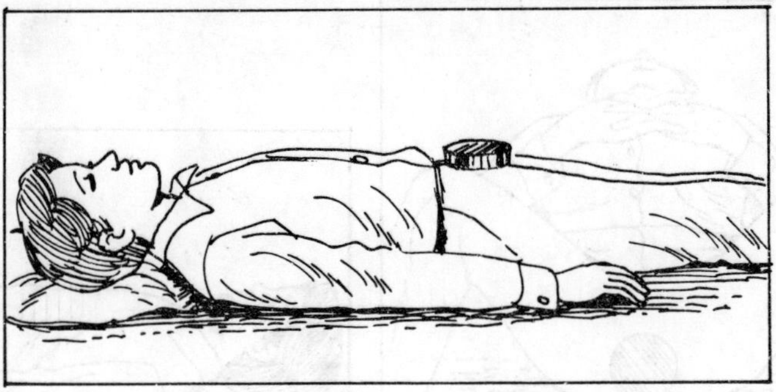

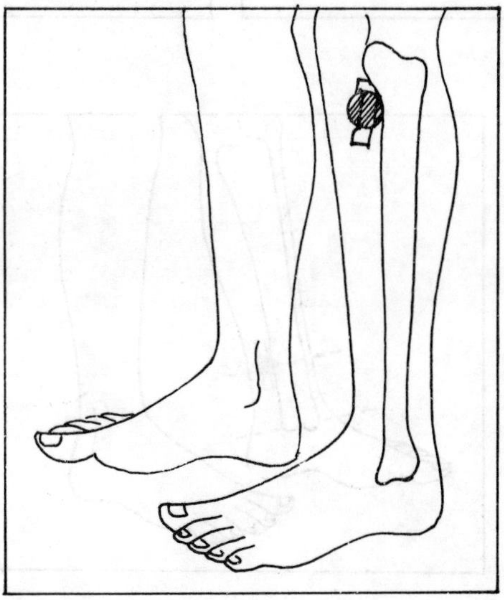

**Magnetic treatment :** (1) The **north pole** of a moderately strong magnet should be applied to the pubic area for 15-30 minutes, 2-3 times a day. (2) The **north pole** of a small magnet should be stuck to the outer aspect of the leg, just below the knee, on the prominently seen bone.

### (3) Prolapse of the uterus :

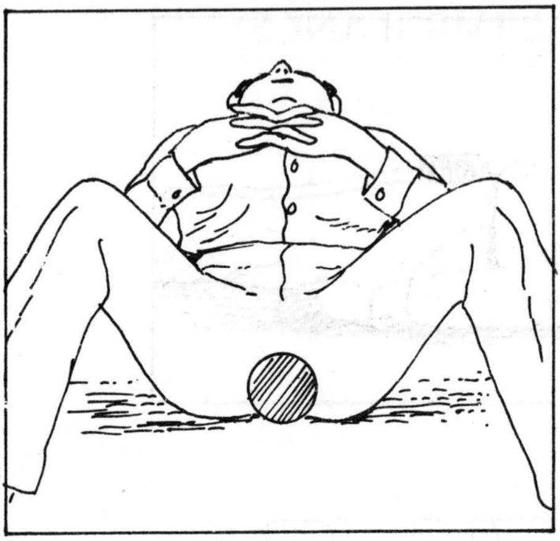

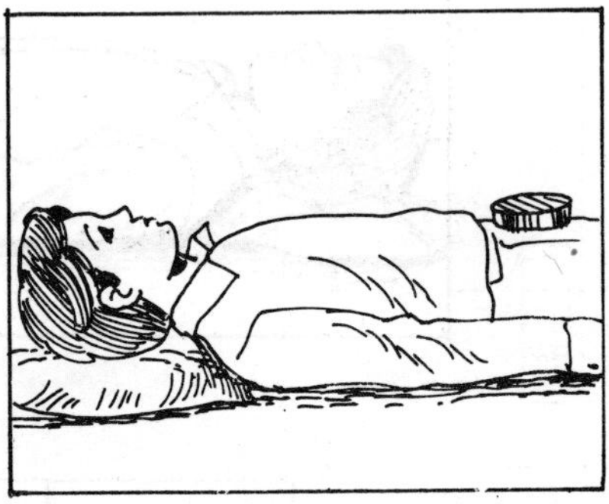

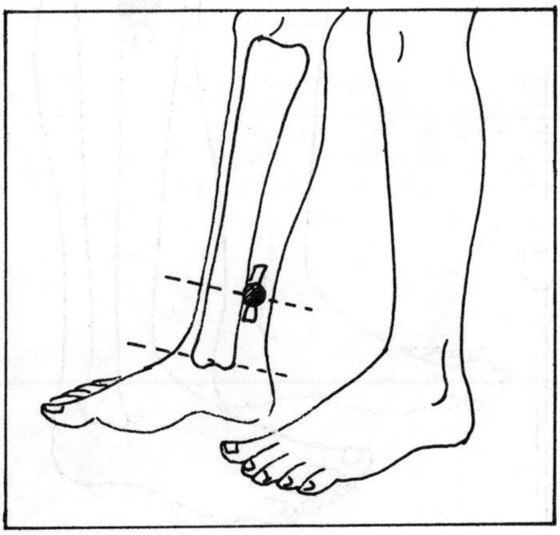

**Magnetic treatment :** (1) The **north pole** of a moderately strong magnet should be applied to the perineum (the part between the genitals and the anus) for 15-30 minutes, 2-3 times a day. (2) The **north pole** of a medium power magnet should be applied to the pubis, for 15-30 minutes, 2-3 times a day. (3) The **north pole** of a small magnet should be stuck to the inner apsect of the leg, four finger-breadths above the inner prominence of the ankle bone. (4) Magnetised water should be drunk 4-5 times a day.

# 26. DISORDERS OF ENDOCRINE GLANDS (HORMONAL IMBALANCE)

**(1) Diabetes :**

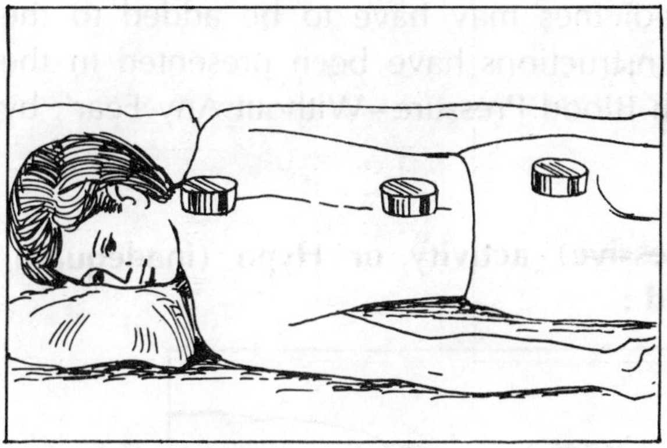

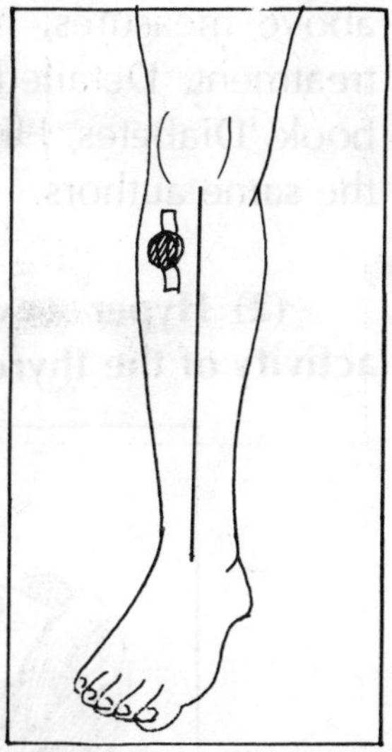

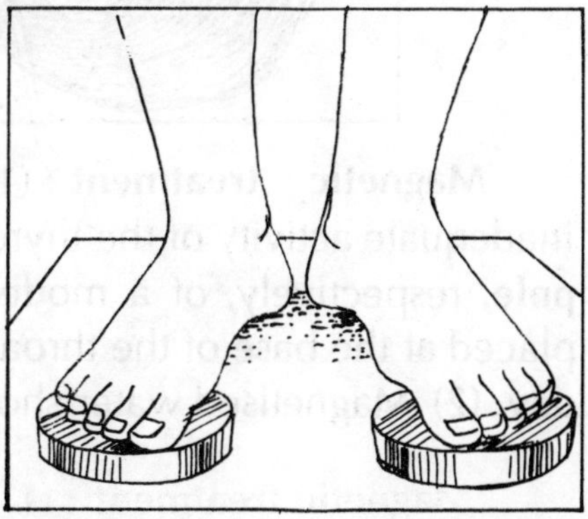

**Magnetic treatment** : (1) The **north** and the **south poles** of strong magnets should be placed side by side on the middle of the back, for 30-45 minutes, 2-3 times a day (preferably an hour after meals or breakfast). (2) The right palm (or sole) and the left palm (or sole) should be placed on the **south** and the **north poles,** respectively, of strong magnets for 15-20 minutes, once or twice a day. (3) The **north pole** of a small magnet should be stuck on the leg four finger-breadths below the lower margin of the round knee-bone. (4) Magnetised water should be drunk 4-5 times a day.

**Note :** Diet should be corrected. Exercises should be taken regularly. If the disease is not controlled adequately with the above measures, medicines may have to be added to the treatment. Detailed instructions have been presented in the book 'Diabetes, High Blood Pressure–Without Any Fear', by the same authors.

**(2) Hyper (excessive) activity or Hypo (inadequate) activity of the thyroid :**

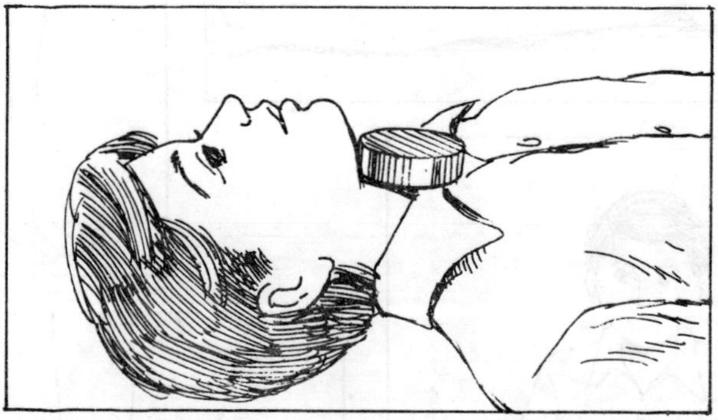

**Magnetic treatment :** (1) In case of excessive or inadequate activity of the thyroid gland, the **south** or the **north pole,** respectively, of a moderately strong magnet should be placed at the base of the throat, for 15-30 minutes, 2-3 times a day. (2) Magnetised water should be drunk 4-5 times a day.

## 27. DISORDERS OF CHILDREN

### (1) Chicken-pox; measles; mumps :

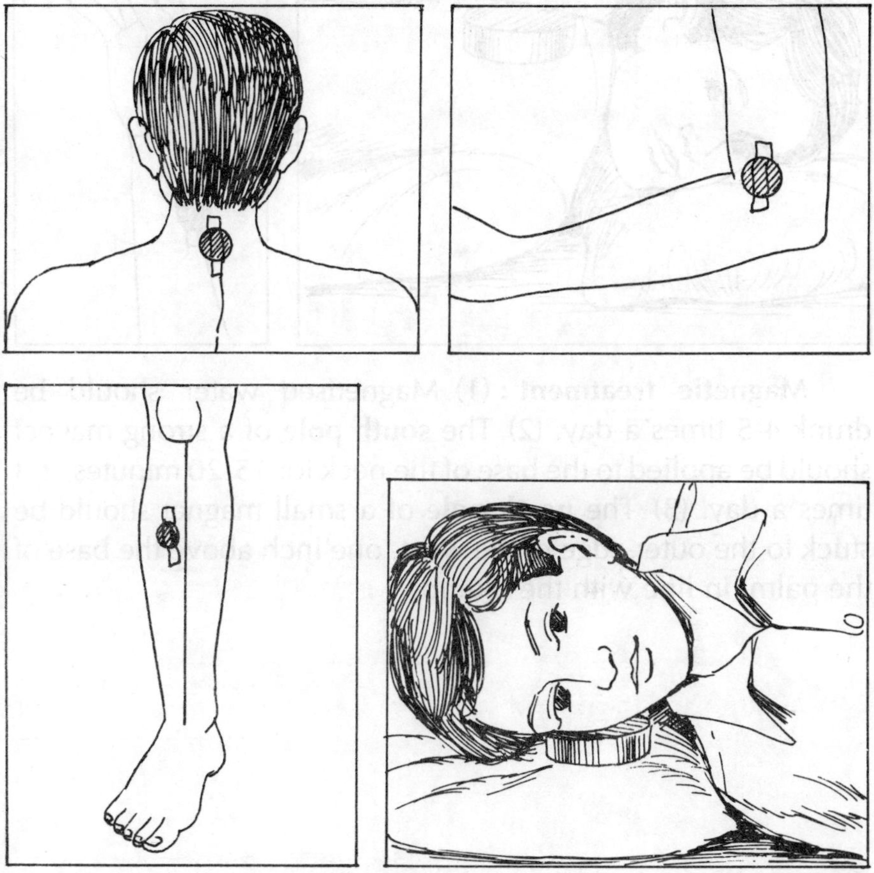

**Magnetic treatment :** (1) Magnetised water should be drunk 4-5 times a day. (2) The **north pole** of a small magnet should be stuck (with sticking plaster) to the following three places : (a) below the most prominently seen neck-vertebra after the head is bent forward (b) at the outer end of the elbow crease after the elbow is half bent (c) four finger-breadths below the lower border of the round knee bone (3) In mumps, the **south pole** of a strong magnet should be applied to the affected cheek, for 15-30 minutes, 2-3 times a day.

**(2) Whooping cough :**

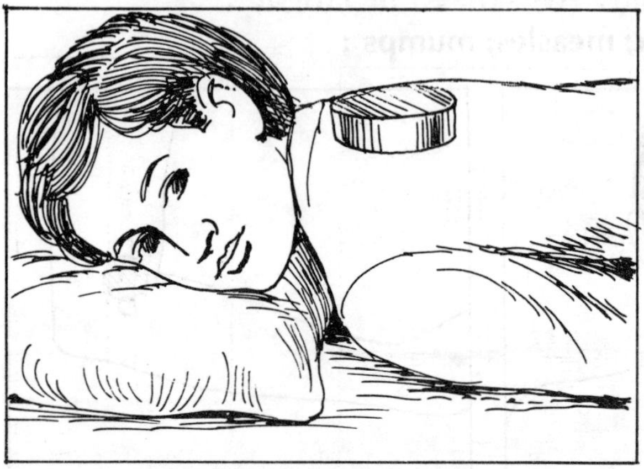

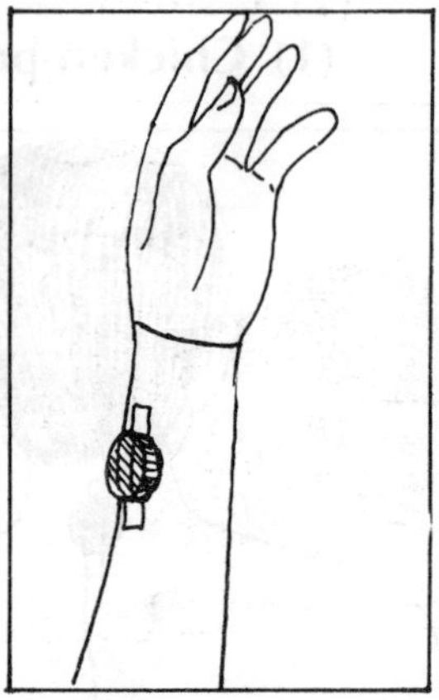

**Magnetic treatment :** (1) Magnetised water should be drunk 4-5 times a day. (2) The **south pole** of a strong magnet should be applied to the base of the neck for 15-20 minutes, 2-3 times a day. (3) The **north pole** of a small magnet should be stuck to the outer edge of the wrist, one inch above the base of the palm, in line with the thumb.

# 28. OTHER COMMON DISORDERS

## (1) General debility (weakness) or fatigue :

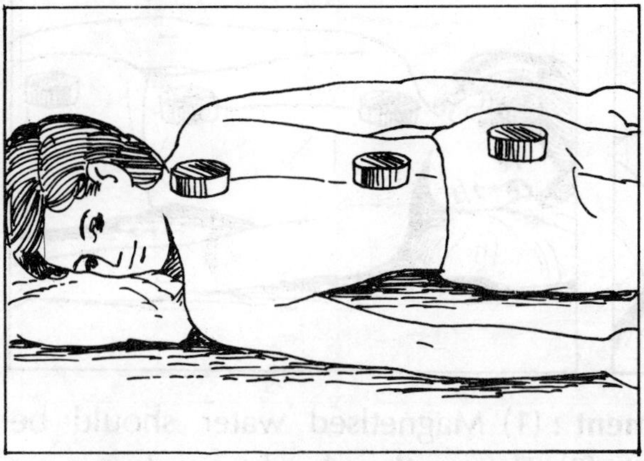

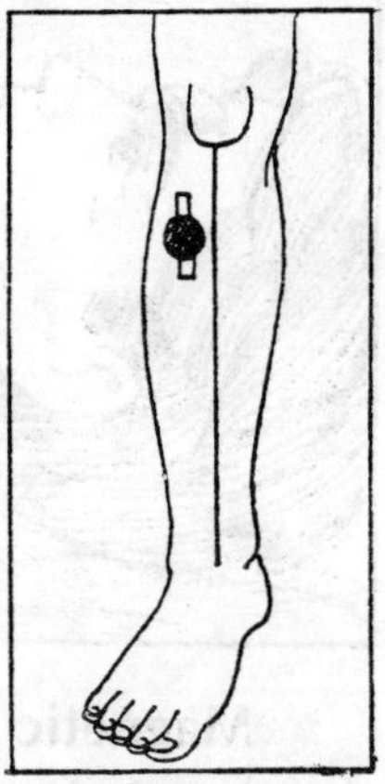

**Magnetic treatment :** (1) Magnetised water should be drunk 4-5 times a day. (2) The **north poles** of strong magnets should be placed on three parts of the vertebral column : at the lower end of the spine, parallel to the navel and at the lower tip of the spine for 15-30 minutes, once or twice a day. (3) The **north pole** of a small magnet should be stuck to the leg, four finger-breadths below the lower margin of the round knee bone.

## (2) Forgetfulness; loss of memory :

**Magnetic treatment :** (1) The **north pole** of a weak magnet should be placed on the forehead, for 15-20 minutes, 2-3 times a day. (2) Magnetised water should be drunk 4-5 times a day.

**(3) Loss of hair; baldness; alopecia; graying of hair :**

**Magnetic treatment :** (1) Magnetised water should be drunk 4-5 times a day. (2) The **south pole** of a weak magnet should be applied to the forehead, for 15-20 minutes, 2-3 times a day. (3) The **north poles** of strong magnets must be placed on three parts of the vertebal column : at the base of the neck, parallel to the navel and at the lower end of the spine for 15-30 minutes, once or twice a day. (4) The scalp should be lightly massaged with magnetised oil.

**(4) Giddiness :**

**Magnetic treatment :** (1) The **south pole** of a weak magnet should be applied to the forehead till giddiness is relieved. If giddiness recurs time and again, the above treatment should be repeated 2-3 times a day, for 15-20 minutes each time. (2) Magnetised water should be drunk 4-5 times a day.

**(5) Excessive perspiration :**

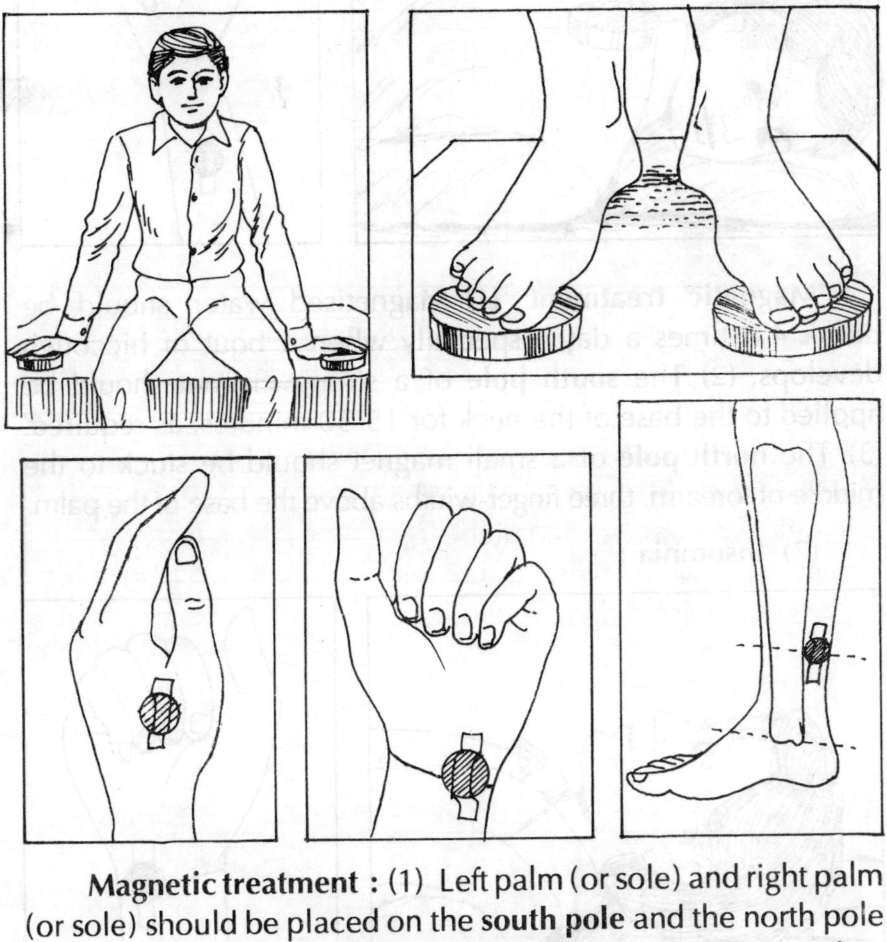

**Magnetic treatment :** (1) Left palm (or sole) and right palm (or sole) should be placed on the **south pole** and the north pole of strong magnets for 15-20 minutes, once or twice a day. (2) The **north poles** of three small magnets should be stuck to the following three parts of the body : on the muscular prominence between the thumb and the first finger, on the inner end of the palm crease in line with the little finger and four finger-breadths above and two finger-breadths to the rear of the inner prominence of ankle bone (see the figure). (3) Magnetised water should be drunk 4-5 times a day.

**(6) Hiccough :**

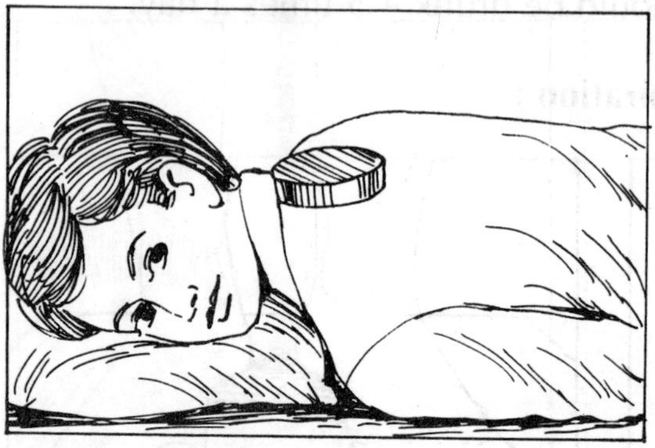

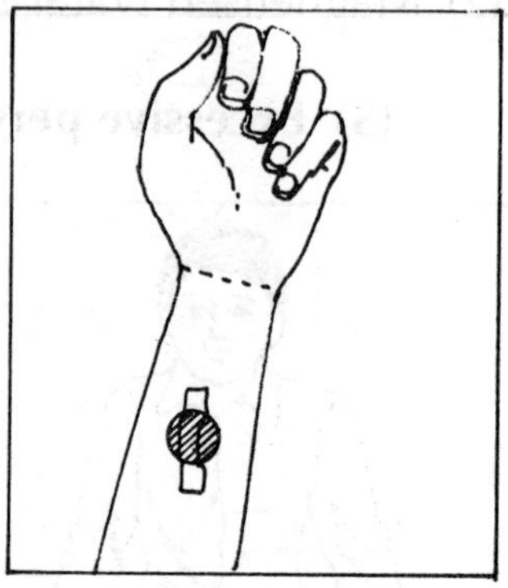

**Magnetic treatment :** (1) Magnetised water should be drunk 4-5 times a day, especially when a bout of hiccough develops. (2) The **south pole** of a strong magnet should be applied to the base of the neck for 15-30 minutes, as required. (3) The **north pole** of a small magnet should be stuck to the middle of forearm, three finger-widths above the base of the palm.

**(7) Insomnia :**

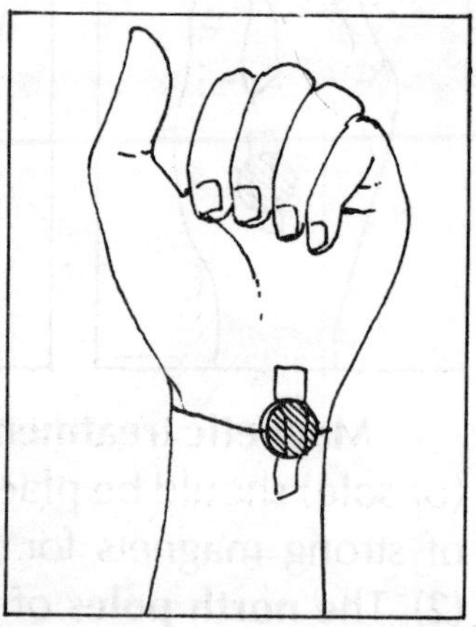

**Magnetic treatment :** (1) The **south pole** of a weak magnet should be applied to forehead for 15-20 minutes, 2-3 times a day (once while going to sleep). (2) The **north pole** of a small magnet should be stuck to the inner end of wrist crease, in line with the little finger. (3) Magnetised water should be drunk 4-5 times a day.

**(8) Allergy :**

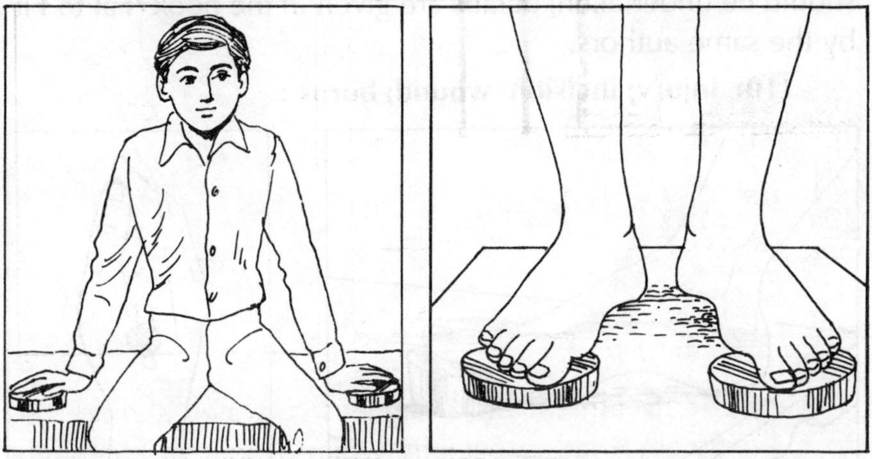

**Magnetic treatment :** (1) Magnetised water must be drunk 4-5 times a day. (2) Right palm (or sole) and left palm (or sole) should be placed on the **north** and the **south poles,** respectively, of strong magnets, for 30-45 minutes, once or twice a day.

**Note :** To avoid the allergic reaction, one should stay away from the harmful substance, if known.

**(9) Obesity; excessive weight :**

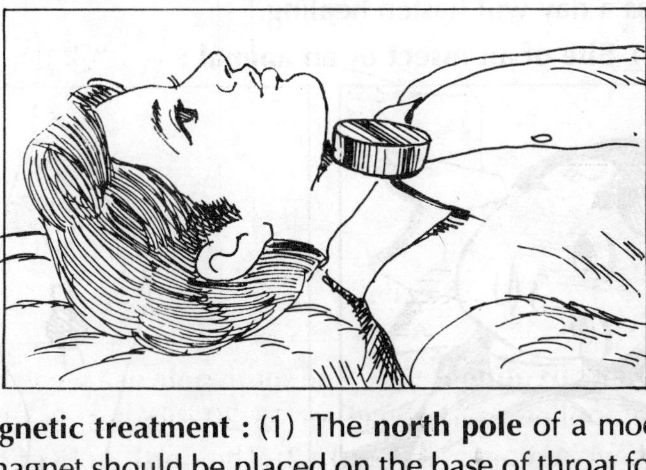

**Magnetic treatment :** (1) The **north pole** of a moderately strong magnet should be placed on the base of throat for 15-30 minutes, 2-3 times a day, preferably about half an hour after meals or breakfast. (2) Magnetised water must be drunk 4-5 times a day.

**Note :** For weight reduction, dieting and exercise, too, should be undertaken; details are given in the book 'Fat to Fit', by the same authors.

**(10) Injury; incision; wound; burns :**

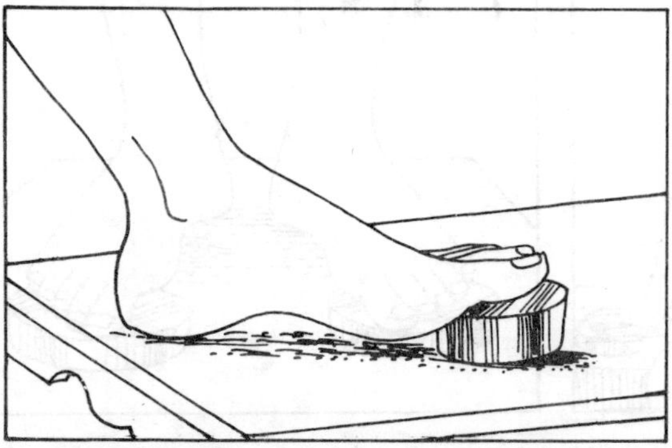

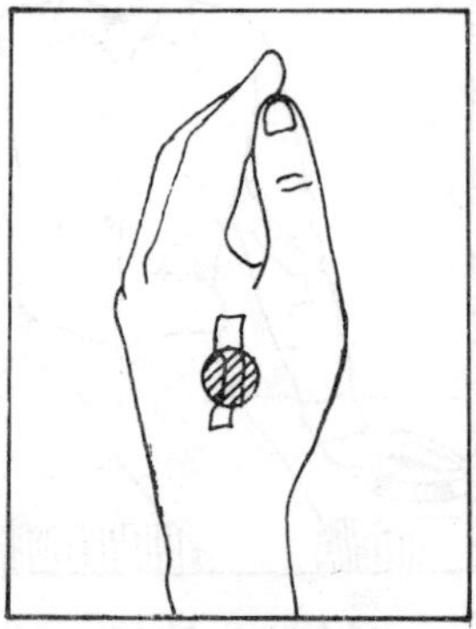

**Magnetic treatment :** (1) Bleeding can be controlled and pain relieved by applying the **south pole** of a strong magnet to the affected part for 30-45 minutes. The treatment can be repeated 2-3 times a day. (2) The **north pole** of a small magnet should be stuck to the muscular prominence between the thumb and first finger. (3) After two-three days, the use of the **north pole** of a strong magnet on the affected part for 15-30 minutes, 2-3 times a day will hasten healing.

**(11) Bite of an insect or an animal :**

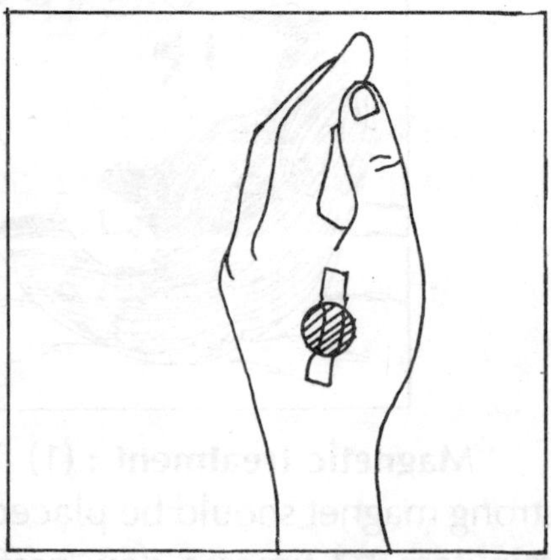

**Magnetic treatment :** (1) The **south pole** of a strong magnet should be applied to the affected part for 15-20 minutes, 2-3

times a day. (2) If there is a lot of pain, the **north pole** of a small magnet should be stuck on the muscular prominence between the thumb and the first finger.

**(12) Tumour; Cancer :**

**Magnetic treatment :** (1) The **south pole** of a strong magnet should be kept on the part affected with tumour for 45-60 minutes, 2-3 times a day. (2) The **north poles** of strong magnets should be placed on the following 2 or 3 parts of the vertebral column : at the base of the neck, parallel to the navel, at the lower end of the spine, for 15-45 minutes, 2-3 times a day. The **north pole,** however, should not be placed anywhere near the tumour. (3) Magnetised water should be drunk 4-5 times a day.

**Note :** In the treatment of cancer, diet also has an important role to play. For details about diet, the reader is advised to read two books 'Juice-Diet for Perfect Health' and 'Wheat Grass Therapy' by the same authors.

**(13) Fever (common fever, influenza, malaria, typhoid etc.) :**

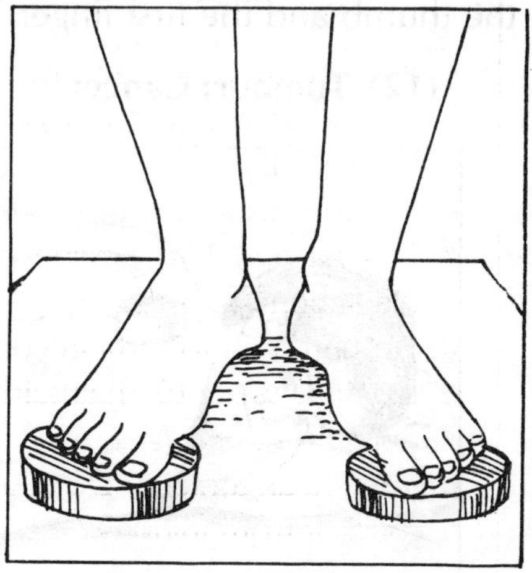

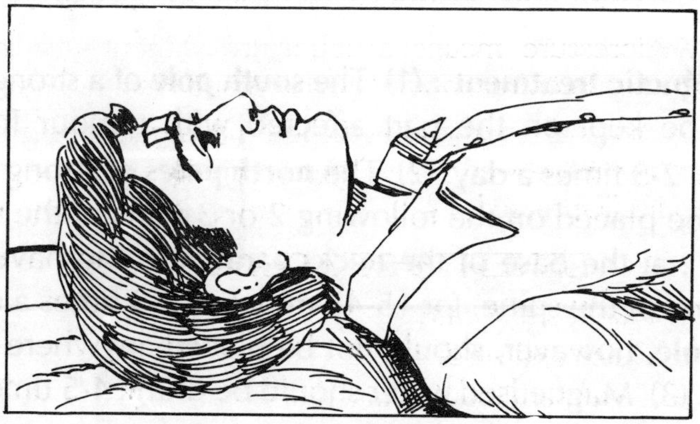

**Magnetic treatment :** (1) Right palm (or sole) and left palm (or sole) should be placed on the **north** and the **south poles,** respectively, of strong magnets for 15-30 minutes, 2-3 times a day. (2) The **south pole** of a weak magnet should be applied to the forehead for 15-30 minutes, 2-3 times a day. (3) Magnetised water should be drunk 4-5 times a day.

**Note :** Fever is not an independent disease, but a mere symptom of some other disease. Therefore, diagnosing the root cause and treating it is also called for.

# BE YOUR OWN DOCTOR WITH ACUPRESSURE

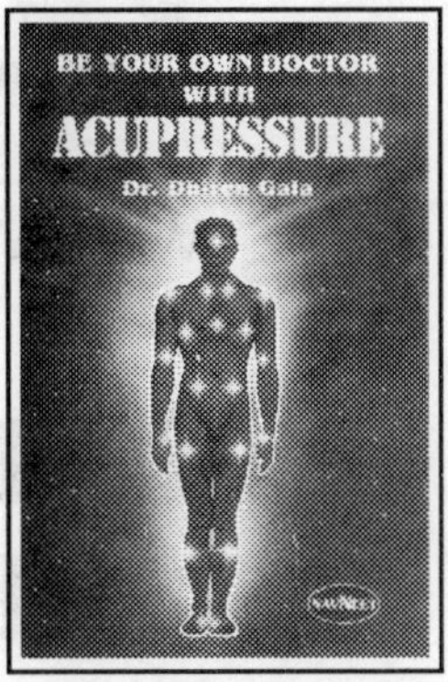


- Are you tired of medicines?
- Is your disease such that cannot be cured by medicines?
- Do you want to prevent illness?
- Do you want to get rid of bad habits (addictions)?
- Do you wish to remain young forever?
- Do you want to maintain your sexual ability for a longer time?
- Are you an athlete? Do you want to save yourself from injuries?

**Then you cannot do without Acupressure**

Acupressure means acupuncture without needles. This therapy has been recognized by the World Health Organization.

In Acupressure therapy, the internal organs of the body are favourably influenced when specific points on the skin are methodically pressed.

## BENEFITS OF ACUPRESSURE

- Painless and safe
- Quick and sure
- Treatment may be taken at home
- Free from harmful side-effects
- No expense – not a single paisa
- Very simple – even a child can learn it

'Be your own doctor' is the only book which gives complete, authentic and scientific information regarding acupressure in simple language, delightful style and through numerous photographs.

NAVNEET

E 4

- Do you take your eyes and vision for granted?
- Have you delegated their well-being to chance?
- Do you ignore the early warning signs of future visual defects or wear glasses without seeking out the real source of the problem?

**Then you are asking for trouble.**

IN FACT YOU CAN CHANGE THE WAY YOU SEE–FOR THE BETTER
by the book

# VISION TRAINING PROGRAMME

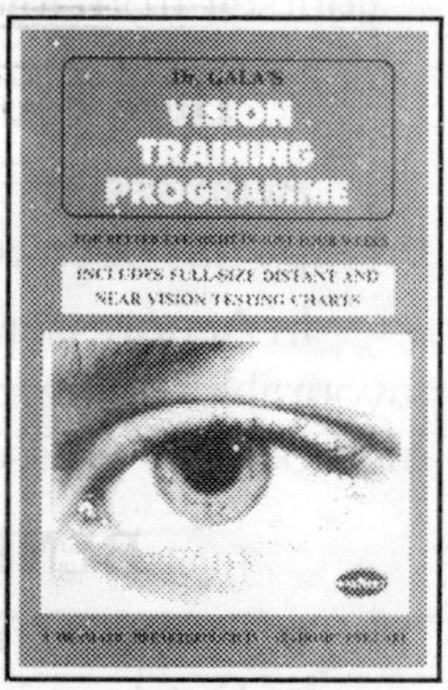


A person's relations with others, his occupation, his personality, his life-style, his success and most other things in life depend upon efficient eyes and good vision. Caring for eyes should be every person's foremost responsibility.

- If your eyes tire or water easily,
- If you can't tolerate even mild sunshine,
- If you wish to learn how to correctly use or rest your eyes,
- If you wish to increase your visual perception and fexibility,
- If you wish to make reading a pleasure again,
- If you wish to lessen your dependence on glasses,
- If you wish to prevent visual problems,
- If you wish to detect and correct your children's eye-problems early and effectively,

**THEN THIS IS THE BOOK FOR YOU.**

**YOU JUST CAN'T IGNORE THE EYE-OPENING FACTS PRESENTED HERE**

NAVNEET

E 10